DORA and LSI Banks

Oliver Michelmann

DORA and LSI Banks

Proportionality Put to the Test

Springer

Oliver Michelmann
Wirtschaftswissenschaften
Allensbach Hochschule
Isernhagen, Germany

ISBN 978-3-658-52896-6 ISBN 978-3-658-52897-3 (eBook)
https://doi.org/10.1007/978-3-658-52897-3

This book is a translation of the original German edition "DORA und LSI-Banken" by Oliver Michelmann, published by Springer Fachmedien Wiesbaden GmbH in 2026. The translation was done with the help of an artificial intelligence machine translation tool. A subsequent human revision was done primarily in terms of content, so that the book will read stylistically differently from a conventional translation. Springer Nature works continuously to further the development of tools for the production of books and on the related technologies to support the authors.

This Springer imprint is published by the registered company Springer Fachmedien Wiesbaden GmbH, part of Springer Nature.
The registered company address is: Abraham-Lincoln-Str. 46, 65189 Wiesbaden, Germany

Contents

List of Abbreviations

AT	General Section (of MaRisk)
BaFin	Federal Financial Supervisory Authority
BAIT	Supervisory Requirements for IT
BiRD	Banks' Integrated Reporting Dictionary
BSI	Federal Office for Information Security
CMDB	Configuration Management Database
CRD	Capital Requirements Directive
CRR	Capital Requirements Directive
CTI	Cyber Threat Intelligence Data
DORA	Digital Operational Resilience Act
EBA	European Banking Authority
EIOPA	European Insurance and Occupational Pensions Authority
ESMA	European Securities and Markets Authority
EU	European Union
EZB	European Central Bank
FS-ISAC	Financial Services Information Sharing and Analysis Center
ICAAP	Internal Capital Adequacy Assessment Process
IKT	Information and Communication Technology
ILAAP	Internal Liquidity Adequacy Assessment Process
IoCs	Indicators of Compromise
iReF	Integrated Reporting Framework
IT	Information technology
ITS	Implementing Technical Standard
KWG	German Banking Act
LSI	Less Significant Institute
MaRisk	Minimum requirements for risk management

MISP	Malware Information Sharing Platform
MW	Mean
NIS2	Network and Information Security Directive 2
PSD2	Payment Services Directive 2
RTS	Regulatory Technical Standard
SD	Standard deviation
SI	Significant institution (total assets of over 30 billion euros)
SIEM	Security Information and Event Management
SLA	Service Level Agreement
SREP	Supervisory Review and Evaluation Process
SSM	Single Supervisory Mechanism
TIBER	Threat Intelligence-Based Ethical Red Teaming
TLPT	Threat-led penetration tests

List of Figures

1 Introduction

"The calibration of financial regulation must not be weakened. Instead, we need less complexity in regulation and more proportionality."[1]
—Mark Branson, President of BaFin, Annual Press Conference on May 14, 2024

In recent years, the density of regulation in the European financial sector has reached a level that is increasingly being critically examined, particularly by the supervisory authorities themselves. In his plea for a regulatory practice aimed at simplification, the President of the Federal Financial Supervisory Authority (BaFin) emphasizes the structural disadvantage faced by smaller institutions due to the current complexity of the financial market, thereby highlighting a barrier for new market entrants. According to Branson, a streamlining and removal of overlaps in European regulations is necessary, without compromising the underlying level of security. This assessment reflects a reality that small and medium-sized credit institutions have been facing for years.[2] The focus here is on complex regulatory requirements arising from the interaction between various capital regimes. These include the CRR/CRD, the governance requirements of MaRisk, the technical minimum standards of BAIT, as well as additional requirements in the areas of sustainability reporting and anti-money laundering. The multi-layered regulatory burden results in increased financial expenditure and a growing need for personnel and technical resources. Often, however, there is a mismatch between the administrative effort and the institution-specific risk profile. The implementation of the DORA Regulation (EU 2022/2554) could further

[1] Branson, 2024.
[2] See Rocholl et al., 2017, pp. 3–17.

O. Michelmann, *DORA and LSI Banks*,
https://doi.org/10.1007/978-3-658-52897-3_1

intensify this tension with regard to ICT risks. Establishing a uniform minimum standard for all financial market participants is both consistent and necessary in terms of European market integration and in light of increasing threats in the areas of cybersecurity, data integrity, and digital dependency on service providers. According to the ECB and EBA, the number of incidents has risen significantly in recent years, and the potential systemic impacts can be considerable. It should be noted that despite the proportionality principle anchored in Art. 4, DORA does not provide for a profound systematic differentiation based on institution-specific characteristics such as size, complexity, or business model. Rather, the requirements apply to all supervised institutions, regardless of whether they are a systemically important large institution or a locally operating LSI (Less Significant Institution). An international comparison shows that in the United States, for example under the "Tailoring Rule" approach, regulatory relief for smaller institutions is increasingly being discussed even in the area of IT and compliance requirements.[3] The EU, on the other hand, is pursuing a far-reaching harmonization and expansion of regulatory obligations with DORA. As a result, LSIs in particular are faced with the challenge of implementing highly complex requirements that have so far been discussed primarily in the context of large, highly interconnected institutions.

1.1 Initial Situation and Context

With the entry into force of the DORA Regulation, a regulatory framework has been established that, for the first time at the European level, provides for comprehensive and cross-sector regulation of ICT risks in the financial sector. The aim is to increase the resilience of financial infrastructure to digital threats and to implement a consistent minimum level of ICT security within the European Union. DORA is directly applicable and obliges not only credit institutions but also insurance companies, payment service providers, asset management companies, and other financial market participants to implement a defined catalogue of measures. As an integral part of the EU Digital Finance Package published in 2020, DORA is intended as a targeted response to the increasing digitalization of the financial sector.[4] The present package of measures aims to establish

[3] See Siems, 2025, pp. 1–44.

[4] See Janciute, 2025, pp. 145–154.

a European strategy to promote innovation, competitiveness, and security in the financial sector. Within the Digital Finance Package, DORA plays a key role as it provides a cross-sector, directly applicable regulatory framework for digital operational resilience and thus offers a regulatory response to the growing dependence on information and communication technologies as well as to new digital threat scenarios. The implementation of DORA takes place particularly in the context of the German supervisory regime, which is already characterized by a high density of regulation. There is already a complex network of national and European requirements for governance, security, and continuity, formed by provisions such as BAIT, the EBA Guidelines on ICT and security risk management, MaRisk, and sector-specific IT frameworks. DORA not only expands this spectrum in terms of content, but also tightens the requirements for documentation, traceability, and accountability. This starting point creates a field of tension between the legitimate goal of ensuring regulatory resilience and practical feasibility, especially for smaller institutions. The so-called LSIs, which make up a significant part of the banking sector in Germany, often have limited personnel, financial, and technical resources and are classified under the Single Supervisory Mechanism (SSM) as non-significant institutions within the meaning of Art. 6 para. 4 SSM Regulation. A credit institution is considered significant, among other things, if it has a balance sheet total of more than €30 billion, operates across borders, or is classified as systemically important.[5] Supervision of LSI institutions in Germany is the responsibility of BaFin in cooperation with the Deutsche Bundesbank. Despite their smaller size, they represent a stability-relevant component of the German banking sector due to their nationwide presence, customer proximity, and role in lending to SMEs. At the same time, however, they are particularly vulnerable to regulatory overburden. For these institutions, the implementation of DORA, especially the detailed requirements specified in the RTS and ITS, can represent a business-relevant burden. The discussion about the proportionality principle anchored in Art. 4 DORA is therefore gaining in importance. While the regulation refers to differentiation by size, type, scope, and complexity of an institution, it remains unclear how this differentiation will be concretely operationalized and applied in supervisory practice.[6] At the same time, it must not be overlooked that the technological reality of the financial system has created a new form of vulnerability: cloud dependencies, cyber threats, and the systemic role of ICT third-party providers are risks that no institution can escape. The regulatory response to

[5] See Osman, 2024, pp. 33–167.

[6] See Leusmann, 2023, pp. 73–88.

this development is, from a financial stability perspective, a logical consequence. The context of the issue lies between the poles of a tightening of regulation with high standards and the question of a practical, proportionate implementation, especially for smaller institutions that are exposed to steadily increasing implementation pressure.

1.2 Objective of the Thesis

The present master's thesis aims to systematically analyze the impact of the DORA Regulation on LSIs in Germany and to assess it in light of the proportionality principle anchored in Art. 4 DORA. The study seeks to develop a differentiated understanding of whether and in which areas the requirements of the DORA Regulation result in a disproportionate burden for LSI institutions. This is to be done particularly in relation to previous national supervisory practice (especially BAIT and MaRisk). In this context, it is of particular relevance to identify those DORA components that are characterized by a high operational implementation effort. These include, in particular, ICT risk management, ICT incident reporting, testing of digital operational resilience, and the management and monitoring of third parties. Given the widespread relevance of LSIs for credit provision in Germany and their simultaneously limited operational resources, a central concern of this thesis is to identify potential areas of tension between regulatory objectives and practical feasibility. The aim is not to question the fundamental necessity of sector-wide resilience requirements. Rather, the intention is to examine whether the current regulatory implementation provides sufficient scope for differentiation to take into account the specific starting conditions of smaller institutions. In this context, the thesis pursues a dual research interest. On the one hand, it provides a practice-oriented contribution to the assessment of the operational implementation of DORA in LSI banks; on the other hand, it establishes a scientifically sound basis for the discussion on an adequate application of the proportionality principle within the European regulatory framework. The present analysis is based on a comprehensive theoretical and regulatory review as well as on the evaluation of empirical data collected as part of a structured survey among German LSI institutions. The empirical results obtained in this thesis are intended to illustrate the concrete implementation experiences of the institutions and to derive practically feasible recommendations for action for targeted clarification or adjustment of existing requirements. The combination of a theoretical-conceptual classification and empirical validation aims to generate added value for institutions in dealing with DORA and to contribute to the further development of European regulatory practice. Both the regulatory objectives and the operational reality of German LSI banks are taken into account.

1.3 Research Questions and Hypotheses

Based on the previously outlined objectives of this thesis, the overarching research question is developed as to what specific challenges these institutions face in the practical implementation of the DORA Regulation and how these can be addressed from the perspective of proportionality. The guiding question is explored in several dimensions of analysis, each relating to different substantive focuses of the DORA Regulation. The analysis particularly identifies the regulatory areas perceived by the affected institutions as especially resource-intensive. Another focus is on evaluating the implementation effort associated with DORA compared to the previous BAIT regulation. In addition, the uncertainties in interpretation and scope for interpretation from the perspective of the institutions are identified. At the same time, attention is paid to measures already implemented as well as potential clarifications or reliefs that could contribute to increasing implementation efficiency. The study will also analyze whether there are discrepancies in the perceived burden among different types of LSIs. Such differences could, for example, be identified depending on the size of the institution, the degree of digitalization, or the business model. In view of this, several testable hypotheses are formulated in this thesis. The hypothesis that LSI banks associate the transition from BAIT to DORA with a significantly higher administrative and organizational effort is put forward as the first hypothesis. Furthermore, it is assumed that, in particular, the requirements for critical ICT service providers and the management of outsourcing relationships are perceived as especially challenging. It is also anticipated that smaller LSIs are subject to greater implementation pressure than larger LSIs. Another focus of the investigation is the newly introduced reporting obligations for ICT incidents, which are considered to entail significant operational effort. Furthermore, it is assumed that there is a particular desire for regulatory clarification, especially in the areas of documentation, reporting, and audit requirements. These questions will be answered on the basis of an empirical study, the methodological approach of which will be explained in more detail in the forthcoming methodology chapter. The aim is to use a structured and hypothesis-driven analysis to provide a differentiated picture of the practical implementation experiences of LSIs and to draw well-founded conclusions for an appropriate design of the proportionality principle within the framework of DORA regulation.

1.4 Structure of the Thesis

This master's thesis is divided into six main chapters that build on each other in terms of content. Following the introduction, which outlines the topic, presents the objectives, and formulates the central research questions and hypotheses, the second chapter provides a systematic presentation of the regulatory framework. Here, the conceptual basis of the thesis is set out, the idea of proportionality in banking supervision is discussed, and the development of ICT-related supervisory requirements is presented. In addition, the central contents of the DORA Regulation are addressed thematically. The third chapter is devoted to the methodology of the empirical study and describes the chosen research approach, operationalization, as well as the implementation and evaluation of the survey. Furthermore, the fourth chapter presents the empirical results of the study. It first shows the general perception of the DORA requirements in the surveyed institutions and then identifies the main areas of burden in the individual subject areas. In addition, the factors influencing the perceived burden are analyzed and classified in terms of their significance for the proportionality principle. Building on these results, the fifth chapter develops proportional design approaches that provide concrete starting points for a target group-oriented implementation of DORA. Strategic implications are also derived to increase the effectiveness of regulation from an efficiency perspective. The final sixth chapter summarizes the key findings, derives practice-oriented recommendations for action, and discusses both methodological limitations and perspectives for further research.

Regulatory Framework 2

The regulatory framework forms the foundation of this work and defines the legal and supervisory requirements within which the analysis is conducted. At the center is DORA as the key European regulation aimed at strengthening the digital resilience of the financial sector. The following sections explain its origins, objectives, and structure, and relate it to existing regulatory frameworks. This contextualization reveals both the regulatory interfaces and potential overlaps that are crucial for understanding the empirically examined questions of proportionality.

2.1 Proportionality in Banking Supervision

The regulation and supervision of credit institutions in Europe is based on largely harmonized regulatory frameworks designed with the goal of creating a single internal market for financial services. This harmonization, for example through the so-called "Single Rule Book," is, however, in tension with the institutional and structural diversity of the European banking sector. In Germany, which is characterized by a historically evolved, highly decentralized banking structure, the question is particularly relevant as to how uniform supervisory requirements can be applied in a way that does justice both to the systemic objectives of financial stability and to institutional diversity.[1] In the German administrative context, this idea of proportionality is supplemented by the concept of "dual proportionality." According to this concept, supervisory requirements must be tailored to the

[1] See Reinert, 2018, pp. 62–83.

O. Michelmann, *DORA and LSI Banks*,
https://doi.org/10.1007/978-3-658-52897-3_2

size and complexity of an institution as well as its risk profile. This principle is of central importance, especially in the context of Section 25a KWG and the administrative regulations based on it, such as the Minimum Requirements for Risk Management (MaRisk).[2]

The practical implementation of the proportionality principle takes place at several regulatory levels. At the EU level, the ECB is responsible for the direct supervision of SIs within the framework of the Single Supervisory Mechanism, while the supervision of LSIs formally remains with the national supervisory authorities. However, the ECB coordinates this area through overarching guidelines and methodologies, aiming for harmonization. Tensions become particularly apparent in the interaction between European central supervision and nationally shaped banking structures. Countries such as France or the Netherlands have highly concentrated banking markets, whereas the German banking sector is characterized by a large number of smaller, locally rooted credit institutions whose business models differ significantly from those of SIs.[3] This structural peculiarity necessitates a differentiated supervisory practice, which in Germany is realized through a dedicated interpretation of the proportionality principle in day-to-day supervision. A key instrument for implementing this principle is the MaRisk, in which the concept of double proportionality is explicitly anchored. In AT 1 para. 2 of MaRisk, it is emphasized that the design of risk management and risk control processes must take into account the nature, scope, complexity, and risk content of an institution's business activities. In this context, particular attention should be paid to the new MaRisk circular from November 2024, which introduced targeted reliefs for smaller, less complex institutions. These reliefs include, for example, the derivation of risk-bearing capacity, the granularity of internal processes, or the requirements for risk data aggregation.[4] The modifications made not only reflect an administrative relief but also manifest regulatory recognition that smaller institutions cannot and need not manage their risks with the same instrumental effort as large banks. At the European level, the SREP methodology (Supervisory Review and Evaluation Process) also demonstrates a formal application of proportionality. The classification of institutions into four different supervisory categories, from systemically important large banks to small regional institutions, is associated with graduated requirements regarding

[2] See Hille, 2018, pp. 50–60.

[3] See Boss et al., 2020, pp. 51–70.

[4] See BaFin, 2024a.

the intensity, frequency, and level of detail of the review.[5] It can be observed that empirical evidence in numerous studies and professional articles indicates that the actual implementation of this differentiated approach is not consistently successful.[6] Especially in the context of ICT requirements, there is a de facto equal treatment of all institutions, which can lead to disproportionately high burdens for smaller entities. Studies have already shown that the relative costs and personnel resource requirements for small institutions increase significantly compared to large entities. These higher costs are due to the lack of economies of scale and specialized departments in small institutions.[7]

This issue becomes particularly relevant when considering digital transformation and the associated regulatory initiatives, especially the DORA regulation. Although Article 4 of DORA generally provides for application in accordance with the proportionality principle, the concrete operationalization of this requirement remains unclear.[8] Particularly in the area of ICT risks and, for example, in requirements for business continuity, incident reporting, or third-party management, there are significant doubts as to whether the intended differentiated approach can actually be realistically implemented.[9] In view of the significant requirements for standardization, technical minimum requirements, and sometimes complex organizational specifications, smaller institutions face the question of whether these requirements can be implemented without jeopardizing the economic balance of their business model.

Against this background, it can be stated that the principle of proportionality, both legally and economically, represents a central steering criterion for effective and fair banking regulation. In German supervisory practice, this principle is anchored both in theory and in practice, although it is not implemented equally in all areas at the European level.[10] Especially in the context of ICT-related requirements, which reach a new level of regulatory depth through DORA, the question of proportional application plays a critical role. The following sections will therefore address the emergence and development of ICT-related supervisory requirements in order to examine the extent to which the proportionality principle is concretely reflected in this area or whether new challenges arise.

---

[5] See Wolberg, 2020, pp. 54–67.
[6] See Joosen/Lehmann, 2019, pp. 65–90.
[7] See Hackethal/Inderst, 2015, pp. 105–128.
[8] See Clausmeier, 2023, pp. 79–90.
[9] See Gorobet, 2024, pp. 54–63.
[10] See Chiarella, 2025, pp. 17–30.

2.2 Development of Supervisory ICT Requirements

The increasing digitalization of banking has fundamentally changed the requirements for regulatory control mechanisms. What was once considered a technical fringe area has evolved into an independent, highly regulated field of supervision.[11] The regulation of ICT in banks did not develop linearly or in a centrally controlled manner, but rather step by step, with varying depth across countries and initially in a fragmented way. The introduction of Basel II in 2004 marked a decisive regulatory turning point in the consideration of ICT risks. With the establishment of operational risk as a third independent risk category alongside credit and market risks, awareness was raised that IT-related incidents such as system failures, cyberattacks, or process failures could represent a relevant supervisory risk profile in the future. The definition of operational risk as a loss resulting from inadequate or failed internal processes, people, and systems or from external events explicitly included IT components and contributed to integrating their management into institutional risk control. Nevertheless, regulation at the conceptual level was designed in an abstract manner, as concrete requirements for IT governance or information security were not formulated. Further regulatory developments were required for the implementation of these requirements at the national level and thus for the anchoring of IT risks in day-to-day supervision.[12]

In Germany, MaRisk, which came into force in 2005, served as the central instrument for interpreting and implementing the qualitative requirements of Section 25a KWG. Their development was significantly driven by the increased emphasis on institution-specific risk assessment that accompanied Basel II. While Basel II was integrated into the Capital Requirements Directives (CRD I) at the European level, German supervisory law saw the need to systematically anchor not only the quantitative requirements but also the qualitative requirements of the "second pillar" in a uniform administrative regulation. MaRisk was thus intended to provide a uniform and practical specification of what is to be understood as an appropriate business organization under Section 25a KWG.[13] Although IT risks were only implicitly addressed in the original version, for example in the context of technical and organizational equipment in AT 7.2 or in requirements for emergency management, they were already recognized at an early stage as a significant component of the bank's risk system. In supervisory practice, a pragmatic

[11] See Rani et al., 2025, pp. 3–26.

[12] See Pereira, 2018, pp. 17–59.

[13] See Glaser, 2022a, pp. 1–14.

approach to regulatory gaps was observed. Since the early versions of MaRisk did not yet contain in-depth technical requirements, the IT Baseline Protection Catalog of the Federal Office for Information Security (BSI) was often referenced in findings and deficiencies in IT audits. The BSI Baseline Protection thus functioned de facto as a supervisory minimum standard, especially for small and medium-sized institutions that did not have extensive IT departments.[14]

A significant milestone in further development was the publication of the BAIT in 2017. This publication was preceded by a growing realization in supervisory practice that the existing MaRisk regulations, despite their principles-based approach, were no longer sufficient to meet the increasing and increasingly complex requirements for the information technology landscapes of credit institutions.[15] Information technology had evolved from a supporting element to a central infrastructure for virtually all core banking processes. With this regulatory framework, BaFin for the first time explicitly and independently specified the requirements for the design and operation of IT systems in institutions. The BAIT thus represent a binding interpretation of the MaRisk requirements in the context of IT and are divided, among other things, into requirements for IT strategy, information security management, authorization and user management, outsourcing, and emergency management. Due to their strong connection to Section 25a KWG, they became the central benchmark in supervisory IT audits under Section 44 KWG. In contrast to earlier regulations, the BAIT pursued a principles-based approach in which the proportionality principle is explicitly applied. The BAIT emphasize that the nature, scope, and complexity of IT requirements must be proportionate to the size, risk situation, and business model of the respective institution. The implementation of this measure enabled especially smaller entities to achieve a manageable implementation of their IT governance and security structures.[16]

Although the BAIT already enabled systematic IT supervision at the national level, the European level initially remained characterized by fragmented approaches. In 2019, the European Supervisory Authorities published a series of guidelines for the management of ICT risks and cybersecurity. These guidelines cover aspects such as outsourcing, incident reporting, and ICT risk management. However, it should be noted that these requirements are not legally binding

[14] See Bornemann/Brandes, 2017, pp. 357–406.

[15] See Buchmüller et al., 2019, pp. 5–25.

[16] See Glaser, 2022b, pp. 299–317.

and are classified as "soft law." Their implementation in the individual European countries varied in intensity, which hindered European harmonization of IT supervision. Despite promising approaches, their practical impact thus remained limited.[17]

In parallel, the ongoing digitalization and increasing threat landscape, such as targeted cyberattacks or massive system disruptions, have increased regulatory pressure. IT has increasingly been recognized as critical infrastructure, whose failure can jeopardize the functioning of the banking system as a whole. The increased use of cloud services, third-party structures, and platform solutions has created new risks that require a unified regulatory response.[18] National authorities such as BaFin and the Deutsche Bundesbank are therefore increasingly focusing on aspects such as digital resilience and ICT resilience testing. This development gradually led to a political consensus that a cross-sectoral European regulatory framework for ICT-related requirements was needed. This culminated in the adoption of the Digital Operational Resilience Act (DORA) in 2022. DORA constitutes the first fully harmonized European legal framework for the digital operational resilience of the financial sector. The regulation introduces requirements for ICT risk management, incident management, third-party monitoring, penetration testing, and uniform reporting obligations. DORA applies across sectors, i.e., to banks, insurers, investment firms, and many other market participants. The aim is to consolidate previously fragmented regulations, unify supervision, and ensure a consistently high level of security throughout the European financial system. For German institutions, DORA means a far-reaching transition. Although a large number of its contents are functionally compatible with existing requirements from MaRisk and BAIT, DORA results in additional, in some cases significantly more detailed requirements. These are particularly evident in the areas of information obligations, technical minimum standards, and the control architecture for ICT third-party providers.[19]

[17] See Kourmpetis, 2022, pp. 211–226.

[18] See Kudinova et al., 2025, pp. 466–483.

[19] See Ananieva/Zhytar, 2025, pp. 20–34.

2.3 DORA—Content and Key Topics

With the ongoing digitalization and increasing interconnectedness of the financial sector, financial market participants today are more exposed than ever to digital threats. These threats endanger not only the operational continuity of individual companies but also pose potential systemic risks to the entire financial market infrastructure. In this context, DORA represents a significant response by the European Union to these challenges. According to the intention of the regulation, a uniform, cross-sectoral regulatory framework is being pursued, the goal of which is to ensure digital operational resilience in the European financial sector. Another objective is to overcome existing regulatory fragmentation.[20] DORA pursues a comprehensive approach that clearly distinguishes itself from earlier measures such as the EBA Guidelines or the NIS2 Directive. Although NIS2 aims for cross-sectoral protection of critical infrastructures, DORA specifically addresses the operational stability and resilience of the financial system, with particular emphasis on ICT risks. The regulation explicitly recognizes the systemic relevance of digital disruptions and obliges institutions to proactively address these risks before they develop into serious threats to market stability and consumer protection.[21]

The scope of DORA is deliberately broad. In addition to traditional credit and financial institutions, the new regulation also applies to insurers, investment firms, payment service providers, crypto service providers, as well as custodians and settlement institutions. So-called critical ICT third-party providers, such as cloud services or software providers, are also being brought under direct supervisory control for the first time. DORA takes into account the fact that numerous institutions have already outsourced essential functions to external service providers for some time. This dependence on external providers carries the potential for significant chain reactions triggered by disruptions at the service providers.[22] In terms of content, DORA focuses on five key areas, which will be examined in greater depth in the further course of this work: ICT risk management, the management and reporting of ICT-related incidents, testing of digital resilience, dealing with ICT third parties, and cross-sectoral information sharing. Together, these topics form a coherent framework that addresses both technical and organizational aspects of

[20] See Giannino et al., 2023, pp. 32–42.
[21] See Resano, 2022, pp. 57–82.
[22] See Kun, 2024, pp. 1–15.

digital resilience. It is accompanied by consistent monitoring and enforcement at both EU and national levels.[23]

In Germany, BaFin plays a central role in the implementation of DORA. Its responsibilities extend not only to the interpretation and application of the regulations but also to harmonization with existing national frameworks such as BAIT or MaRisk. In this function, it acts as a coordinating body between European requirements and institutional practice, thus making a significant contribution to regulatory coherence.[24] Moreover, DORA embodies a fundamental shift in the way regulatory requirements for digital resilience are formulated. The regulation goes beyond traditional business continuity approaches and requires affected actors to have a comprehensive understanding and management of their digital attack surfaces. As a result, DORA not only contributes to the stabilization of financial markets but also serves as a strategic instrument for strengthening digital sovereignty within the European Union.[25]

2.3.1 ICT Risk Management

ICT risk management constitutes the foundation of the regulatory requirements of the DORA regulation and is of critical importance for the digital operational resilience of financial companies. It addresses organizations' ability to respond to, monitor, mitigate, and recover from digital threats. With DORA, the European Union has created a uniform regulatory framework that obliges all financial entities to establish a robust, systematic, and documented framework for dealing with information and communication technology risks.[26]

The regulation is based on a comprehensive understanding of ICT risks, which include not only technical but also organizational and strategic aspects. According to the common definition, ICT risks can be subdivided into various risk types. Availability risks resulting from failures or disruptions must be considered, as well as security risks, such as those arising from attacks on the confidentiality or integrity of data sets. In addition, change risks caused by inadequate change processes must be taken into account. Not to be forgotten are risks due to data

[23] See Mulligan/Pierides, 2024, pp. 102–118.
[24] See Alugoju, 2024, pp. 911–921.
[25] See Camacho et al., 2024, pp. 2226–2249.
[26] See FMA, 2025, pp. 1–4.

integrity issues or data loss, as well as outsourcing risks from third parties. This typology corresponds both to the EBA framework and to the operational risk dimensions anchored in DORA.[27] The goal is to identify potential risks at an early stage, assess their probability of occurrence and potential impact, and, on this basis, define appropriate control and mitigation measures. In this context, DORA obliges financial entities to establish an independent ICT risk management framework that is formally documented, regularly updated, and embedded in the overarching governance structure. This framework must be anchored both strategically and operationally. The company-specific risk tolerance must be taken into account, and methods for systematic risk analysis and assessment must be provided. This includes setting thresholds for acceptable residual risks as well as defining escalation processes and responsibilities. Since ICT risks are dynamic and evolve in parallel with the pace of technological innovation, DORA also requires continuous monitoring of these risks, which must take into account both internal and external threat scenarios to ensure the timeliness and effectiveness of control mechanisms.[28] DORA's integrative perspective is particularly relevant in this context, as ICT risk management is not understood in isolation but as an integral part of a comprehensive management and control system. The regulation explicitly requires the integration of the framework into existing processes for capital and liquidity management, such as ICAAP and ILAAP. This ensures a linkage with economic risk-bearing capacity and strategic planning.[29] The governance function, especially the role of management and control bodies, plays a central role. This body is responsible not only for formally approving ICT risks but also for actively managing, monitoring, and integrating them into the company's overall strategy. In addition to technical requirements, DORA therefore also demands an organizational rethinking regarding the importance of IT security and digital resilience.[30]

In January 2024, the European Supervisory Authorities published regulatory technical standards (RTS) supplementing the regulation, which specify individual requirements. The RTS can be divided into several sections, including requirements for security policies, access controls, network security, encryption, logging, change management, and dealing with third parties. In this context, a technology-neutral approach proves essential. The established standards do

[27] See Begozzi, 2023, pp. 27–36.
[28] See EBA, 2024, p. 17.
[29] See Igl, 2025, pp. 1–7.
[30] See Scheidl, 2025, pp. 1–4.

not specify particular tools or platforms but set out principles that are applicable to current and future technologies. In addition, the RTS require that risks be addressed not only technically but also organizationally. This can be achieved, for example, through access restrictions, training measures, awareness programs, or structured emergency plans.[31] According to the scientific literature, efficient information security risk management, in addition to the compliance perspective, has a preventive function with regard to internal misconduct and fraud. Through clear processes, comprehensive documentation, access restrictions, and systematic monitoring, manipulation, misuse, or data exfiltration can be made more difficult or detected at an early stage. Empirical studies show that, especially in complex organizations, embedding security awareness in corporate culture and combining technical and procedural protection mechanisms are crucial for sustainable resilience.[32] At the same time, a multitude of challenges manifest themselves in practical implementation. Quantifying risks in the ICT area, especially non-financial damages, proves to be a complex undertaking. Many organizations still lack suitable measurement tools or the necessary know-how to systematically assess digital risks. In addition, the high dynamics of external threats must be taken into account, which, with the increasing use of cloud services and the outsourcing of critical functions, create new attack surfaces. In this context, DORA calls for the continuous development of protective mechanisms as well as an active engagement with one's own digital attack surface.

2.3.2 ICT-related Incidents

A central component for ensuring digital resilience under the DORA Regulation is therefore the structured management of ICT-related incidents. In view of the growing attack surface of digitalized business processes and the increasing dependence on ICT systems, the professional handling of unplanned events that compromise the security, availability, or integrity of these systems is a regulatory necessity. According to Article 17 of DORA, financial institutions are required to implement processes for the detection, classification, handling, and reporting of ICT-related incidents. The aim is to identify disruptions rapidly, minimize their impact, and implement regulatory reporting obligations as well as internal

[31] EBA, 2024, pp. 19 f.

[32] Mwai, 2025, pp. 36–64.

escalation and recovery processes with precision.[33] The regulation differentiates between general ICT incidents, major ICT-related incidents, and significant cyber threats. The classification of an incident as "major" is tied to a multitude of defined criteria, which have been specified in a regulatory technical standard. Relevant factors include, among others, the number of affected customers or business units, geographical spread, economic impact, downtime, data loss, and reputational risks.[34] These factors are central for classification into prioritized reporting categories to ensure an appropriate response intensity by both the company and the authorities.

To meet regulatory requirements, financial institutions are required to establish comprehensive processes for the early detection and handling of ICT incidents. This includes the implementation of suitable monitoring and logging systems, early warning indicators, and automated notification mechanisms that respond to abnormal system activities. The seamless recording of these incidents, their causes, implemented countermeasures, and recovery activities is not only crucial for compliance reasons but also forms the basis for internal improvement cycles and strategic resilience planning.[35] The requirements also include continuous follow-up and systematic root cause analysis to identify systemic weaknesses or recurring patterns at an early stage. A particularly significant aspect of the regulation concerns the reporting obligations for major ICT-related incidents, as regulated in Article 19 of the DORA Regulation and specified by technical standards. Financial institutions are required to make an initial notification of major incidents within four hours of detection. Structured initial, interim, and final reports must be submitted. The reporting obligations serve not only supervisory purposes but also enable aggregated risk analyses at the European level and more effective threat management by the competent authorities. The information to be submitted includes, among other things, a detailed description of the incident, a breakdown of affected systems, an analysis of customer groups, a record of timelines, an assessment of severity levels, and a list of measures taken for damage limitation and recovery.[36] To optimize the comparability and processing of incoming reports, standardized formats, codes, and reporting categories have been defined. In light of existing reporting obligations under NIS2 or the PSD2 Directive,

---

[33] See European Commission, 2024a, pp. 2–7.

[34] See Sowa, 2025, pp. 48–54.

[35] See Benroider et al., 2023, pp. 570–585.

[36] See Fernandes/Ignaim, 2025, pp. 701–724.

harmonizing these reporting channels presents a particular challenge. According to Article 21, DORA aims to create a centralized European reporting platform. The goal is to reduce the operational burden on companies and enable more efficient data analysis.[37] Meeting DORA requirements in the area of incident management is associated with numerous practical challenges. These include, in particular, the technical and organizational ability to provide valid information within tight timeframes, the parallel management of complex incidents, and coordinated communication with various internal and external stakeholders, especially in incidents involving third parties. Precisely assessing impacts, such as financial losses or reputational damage, also poses a methodological challenge for many institutions. The guidelines published by the EBA for estimating costs and losses provide methodological support here, for example in distinguishing between direct and indirect incident consequences.[38]

At the same time, the standardized requirements also open up potential for efficiency gains. Companies that are able to digitalize, automate, or support incident management processes with standardized tools benefit from greater transparency, shorter response times, and increased trust from customers and supervisory authorities. The academic discussion also highlights the reputational value of proactive incident communication. An open, structured, and credible response to incidents can even strengthen trust in the affected company.[39] The design and implementation of these requirements thus significantly influence organizations' ability to handle and systematically manage digital disruptions.

2.3.3 Testing Digital Resilience

A central aspect of strengthening digital operational resilience under the DORA Regulation is the structured testing of the digital resilience of financial institutions. Articles 24 to 27 of the Regulation set out the obligation to conduct appropriate tests to ensure the functionality of ICT even under stress conditions or to guarantee rapid recovery. The focus of these tests is not solely on identifying technical vulnerabilities but also extends to evaluating organizational and procedural response mechanisms. The regulatory focus is on establishing a continuous, risk-based testing program tailored to the individual size, risk profile, and

[37] See Frantz et al., 2024, p. 126.

[38] See Arnaoudova/Nisheva-Pavlova, 2023, pp. 25–36.

[39] See Boggini, 2024, pp. 1–8.

complexity of each institution.[40] The testing program is an integral part of the overarching ICT risk management framework and serves to practically verify the effectiveness of prevention, response, and recovery measures in the event of unexpected technical disruptions or cyberattacks. In this context, a diversification of test types can be observed, including classic vulnerability analyses, code reviews, technical end-to-end tests, and controlled penetration tests. Particular attention is paid to the institutions' ability to realistically simulate relevant systems and processes. The aim of this measure is to obtain the most robust picture possible of operational stability.[41]

Of particular regulatory significance are the so-called Threat-Led Penetration Tests (TLPT), which are based on Art. 26 DORA and are mandatory especially for larger institutions with complex system architectures. The methodology of these tests closely follows the European TIBER-EU framework and must be conducted at least every three years under the supervision of the competent authorities. For this purpose, specially authorized external providers are engaged to attempt to penetrate a company's critical systems, based on real threat scenarios. The goal is to identify realistic attack vectors and validate response processes under real-time conditions. However, the mandatory execution of such TLPTs represents a considerable organizational and financial burden. For this reason, DORA explicitly provides that LSIs, especially those below the microenterprise threshold or with a simplified ICT risk management framework, are exempt from this obligation. This illustrates the first expression of the proportionality principle within the Regulation. According to this principle, different regulatory intensities are provided depending on risk exposure.[42]

In addition to the general introduction of these testing obligations, there are some challenges in practical implementation. These include, for example, a lack of internal resources for conducting tests, unclear responsibilities in institutional governance, or difficulties in procuring suitable service providers with the necessary certification and regulatory approval. The methodological heterogeneity of available testing approaches and the often low maturity of integrated test automation also hinder systematic implementation. Especially for institutions with complex IT landscapes and numerous interfaces to third-party providers, coordinating

[40] See EU, 2025, Art. 24.

[41] See AFM, 2024, pp. 1–8.

[42] See Barg/Stargardt, 2024, pp. 1–5.

comprehensive test scenarios poses a significant organizational problem.[43] At the same time, the regulation also reveals potential for relief. The formal establishment of a structured testing program offers the opportunity to transfer previously fragmented testing activities into a holistic, standardized framework. In the long term, this can lead to increased efficiency and consistency in resilience assessment. The implementation of maturity models for test planning and evaluation, as discussed in current academic literature, also enables optimized comparability and management of maturity levels within institutions.[44] Furthermore, it becomes clear that resilience tests should not only serve the formal fulfillment of regulatory requirements but should also be understood as a strategic learning tool. This enables the identification of both technical weaknesses and organizational blind spots. As a consequence, this can strengthen a company's resilience capabilities in the long term.[45]

2.3.4 ICT Third Parties

The increasing dependence of the financial sector on external information and communication technology providers has made the management of ICT third parties one of the central regulatory areas of the DORA Regulation. The present study examines the impact of digitalization on companies' risk profiles. The focus of the analysis is the significant increase in systemic risks caused by disruptions in the supply chain. These risks are primarily due to the outsourcing of essential business processes, the centralization of IT infrastructures, and the growing dependence on a few dominant cloud or platform providers. In light of this, DORA aims to create a uniform, binding, and risk-based framework for the management, control, and documentation of ICT third-party relationships. In line with this intention, all financial entities are to be required to make their dependencies transparent, adapt their risk policies, and restructure their contracts.[46] The requirements for financial institutions concern both organizational and contractual aspects of third-party management. According to Articles 28 to 30 of the Regulation, all institutions are required to develop an ICT third-party strategy that

[43] See Blix et al., 2025, pp. 269–288.

[44] See Grima/Marano, 2021, pp. 1–8.

[45] See Milkau, 2021, pp. 408–425.

[46] See Scott, 2021, pp. 1–24.

systematically regulates the selection, assessment, monitoring, and, if necessary, termination of third-party relationships. This strategy must be integrated into the overarching ICT risk management. Responsibility for adoption and oversight lies with the management board. Particular attention is paid to risk diversification, the definition of critical functions, and the establishment of exit strategies in the event of the loss of individual providers.[47] DORA thus does not rely solely on technical security aspects but also explicitly reinforces the governance responsibility of institutions.

A central element of this regulation is the so-called information register, the maintenance of which is mandatory under Article 28(9) DORA. It is essential that all ICT service contracts are recorded, regardless of whether they involve outsourcing, support services, or ancillary agreements. The technical design has been specified in an ITS, which provides for a total of 15 interlinked table formats with around 100 attributes.[48] In addition to the contracting parties and service descriptions, information on subcontracting, service chains, criticality assessments, and deadlines must also be provided. Another focus is on audit-proof historical archiving of contract data for up to five years after contract termination. Many institutions face practical challenges here, both in terms of data availability from providers and with regard to the internal tool and process landscape for maintaining such registers.[49] Contract design itself is also significantly influenced by DORA. According to the Regulation, contractual agreements with ICT service providers must include specific provisions on security requirements, audit rights, incident reporting, service level agreements, exit scenarios, and the further subcontracting of services. The corresponding minimum requirements have been specified in a separate regulatory technical standard, which also covers, among other things, the involvement of sub-service providers.[50] In this context, it is particularly relevant that DORA no longer differentiates between outsourcing and other service relationships. The obligation for contractual safeguards therefore applies in principle to all ICT services, regardless of their legal qualification. This results in a significant expansion of the scope of compliance requirements, meaning that a large number of contracts previously not considered relevant for supervision are now classified as such.

47 See Avsuvarova, 2023, pp. 1–7.
48 See Wendt, 2024, pp. 1–4.
49 See Riaz/Younas, 2024, pp. 23–33.
50 See European Commission, 2024b, pp. 5–8.

For particularly critical ICT service providers—those whose failure or impairment could lead to systemic risks—DORA also provides for direct supervision by the European supervisory authorities, as regulated in Article 31 et seq. The so-called EU oversight structure allows specific third parties to be designated, which are then subject to their own monitoring and intervention regime. In practice, however, this measure is likely to affect only a few globally active providers. For LSIs, which are the primary focus of this work, these specific rules therefore have only limited direct effect, but they exemplify the direction in which European regulation is moving with regard to supply chain management.[51] Practical implementation is associated with further challenges. These include increased effort for contract review and adjustment, lack of standardization of data formats, insufficient willingness to cooperate on the part of some providers, and the need to implement new digital tools for register maintenance, documentation, and monitoring. Many institutions, especially in the LSI sector, are forced to completely redesign existing processes and undertake a more comprehensive centralization of service provider management.[52] The development of automated governance solutions, such as those possible via CloudGate or comparable platforms, is increasingly seen as a pragmatic solution. A key aspect here is that the complexity of the requirements makes purely manual processing virtually impossible.

At the same time, DORA also creates clear opportunities in third-party management: The obligation to maintain central registers, standardized contract clauses, and the explicit anchoring of exit strategies enables institutions to systematically analyze and reduce their dependencies in the long term. In an environment characterized by increasing concentration risks among hyperscalers such as Microsoft or Google, this can become a strategic advantage.[53]

2.3.5 Information Sharing

The systematic exchange of information on cyber threats represents another integral part of the regulatory framework for digital operational resilience under the DORA Regulation. According to Article 45, DORA for the first time establishes a uniform legal framework across the Union that specifically promotes voluntary

[51] See Busch, 2024, pp. 3–23.

[52] See Aben/Etti, 2023, pp. 67–84.

[53] See Duggan, 2024, pp. 344–350.

information-sharing initiatives among financial institutions to strengthen collective defense capabilities against digital threats. In an increasingly networked financial ecosystem shaped by cyber risks, this form of cooperation is of particular importance, as individual institutions often lack the necessary capacity to independently detect and effectively counter threats.[54]

According to Article 45(1) DORA, financial institutions may voluntarily exchange information and insights about potential or actual cyber threats. The aim of this exchange is to improve threat awareness, shorten response times, and strengthen collective resilience. This includes, in particular, so-called Cyber Threat Intelligence (CTI) data, such as indicators of compromise (IoCs), attack vectors, tactics and methods of attackers, as well as specific information on vulnerabilities, security gaps, and appropriate countermeasures.[55] However, the exchange may only take place within so-called trusted communities, which must have clear governance structures, codes of conduct, and measures to protect trade secrets, personal data, and to comply with competition law. DORA also stipulates that this exchange is not limited to the informal transfer of data but may also include operational measures. According to Article 45(1), joint exercises, tests, and simulations may be conducted among participating institutions to verify the effectiveness of existing response and recovery processes. Such emergency exercises allow the simulation of real threat scenarios in a protected environment and generate institutional learning effects. For smaller institutions, they are a valuable tool for testing their own defense capabilities without having to maintain a full-scale red-teaming or complex testing framework.[56]

A key feature of the DORA regulation on information sharing is its flexibility. Participation in such initiatives is generally voluntary but requires prior registration. It is the responsibility of institutions to inform their supervisory authorities of their entry into and exit from the relevant communities. In this context, the legislator combines informal cooperation mechanisms with regulatory transparency, which serves as an important control function, especially with regard to potential reputational risks or disincentives.[57] In practice, various platforms and organizations already exist that can serve as models for DORA-compliant exchange formats. In Germany, these include the Alliance for Cyber Security

[54] See Schlenker/Waschbusch, 2024, pp. 213–236.

[55] See Pier-Giorgi, 2024, pp. 1–9.

[56] See Buttigieg/Zimmermann 2024, pp. 11–28.

[57] See Bernnat, 2025, pp. 197–215.

or the Cyber Security Sharing and Analytics Association (Cyber Security Sharing and Analytics e. V.), and at the European level, the TIBER-DE Community or the Financial Services Information Sharing and Analysis Center (FS-ISAC). These formats allow for structured information sharing, coordinated creation of situational reports, and technical interoperability. This is achieved, for example, via platforms such as MISP (Malware Information Sharing Platform), which also enables automated real-time data exchange.[58]

At the same time, it must be noted that building such structures is associated with considerable challenges. In addition to organizational effort, legal uncertainties regarding data protection, competition law, and liability issues are particularly noteworthy, which have so far prevented many institutions from actively participating. There is also uncertainty about which information is actually "suitably shareable" or how to deal with different maturity levels within a sharing community.[59] There are also concerns that larger institutions, due to their dominant knowledge advantage, could shape the exchange asymmetrically, while smaller players remain primarily reactive. These concerns must be taken into account in the design of future cooperation formats and addressed through clear governance principles and support measures. Nevertheless, structured information sharing offers significant potential for improving resilience in the financial sector. Shared knowledge about potential threats can lead to faster response times, earlier detection of new attack patterns, and coordinated countermeasures. Empirical research sees this development as an opportunity not only to strengthen technical defense capabilities but also to foster a collective awareness and a culture of prevention.[60]

2.4 Differences from Previous Regulations

With the entry into force of DORA on January 17, 2025, the applicability of the previously valid BAIT in Germany will end. Since its introduction in 2017, BAIT has served as the central regulatory basis for the IT organization of credit institutions, especially in the LSI segment. DORA now establishes a new European legal framework that applies directly as a regulation and brings about EU-wide

[58] See Ositashvili, 2024, pp. 1–20.
[59] See Correia & Gonçalves, 2024, pp. 1–20.
[60] See Gauthier-Maxence, 2024, pp. 1–8.

harmonization of requirements for digital resilience and ICT risk management.[61] A key characteristic of BAIT was its deliberately open wording of many requirements. The design was largely left to the institutions themselves, which had the advantage of a certain flexibility in implementation but also led to uncertainty about the minimum supervisory expectations. Concrete methodological or technical minimum requirements were only specified in BAIT in isolated cases. Only with DORA is a systematic specification implemented in the form of RTS and ITS, which contain detailed requirements for procedures and thresholds. This development marks a fundamental shift toward a more rules-based supervisory approach, with immediate consequences, especially for small and medium-sized institutions. These institutions are now required to critically review and formally underpin existing structures and processes.[62]

A central element of this change is the assignment of responsibility to the management body. Although BAIT in its original version already required that management be responsible for an appropriate IT strategy and its adequate implementation, Article 4 of DORA establishes an explicit auditability of this responsibility. Management bodies are not only required to approve strategic policy documents but also to actively manage and oversee ICT risk management, including resource allocation and budget use. For LSIs, this results in a significant intensification of formal governance requirements, which are no longer limited to operational implementation processes but must be anchored and verifiable at board level.[63] Differences can also be observed in the depth and formalization of ICT risk management. BAIT already requires institution-wide risk management that takes ICT structures into account. This corresponds to the requirements known from the MaRisk elements AT 4.3.1 and AT 7.2.[64] DORA translates these general requirements into a detailed and binding framework, which in Articles 5 to 14 sets out key requirements for asset management, risk assessment, vulnerability management, backup strategies, and internal control procedures. In contrast to the approach under BAIT, where many of these aspects are only addressed indirectly or contextually, under DORA they become independent audit objects with clear documentation obligations. For LSIs, this results in the need for significant adjustments to existing concepts for IT strategy, IT governance, or information security. This includes, for example, the implementation of clear processes

[61] See Teichmann, 2025, pp. 235–285.

[62] See Bauer, 2023, pp. 1–6.

[63] See Carrillo, 2023, pp. 1133–1166.

[64] See Biernat/Maksimovic, 2019, pp. 93–188.

for risk allocation, documentation of protective measures, or the conduct of regular effectiveness checks.[65]

A clear difference exists in the area of incident management. From a BAIT perspective, the implementation of adequate emergency and incident management was already required. In practice, this usually implies the implementation of an ISMS, supplemented by reporting processes and fallback plans. In contrast, DORA not only standardizes processes for incident handling but also introduces, with Articles 15 to 20, a multi-level reporting system that classifies incidents as normal or major and specifies concrete deadlines and formats for reporting to supervisory authorities.[66] In addition, accompanying RTS and ITS further regulate the content requirements for reporting in detail. For LSIs that have so far only organized such reporting channels ad hoc in the context of IT service interruptions, this creates a new, formalized reporting obligation. This requires not only technical infrastructure but also organizational clarity and reporting routines. Unlike BAIT, DORA also prescribes regular testing of digital resilience, with requirements graded according to institution size and complexity. The TLPTs introduced under DORA are, however, primarily aimed at larger and more complex institutions with systemic relevance or high degrees of interconnectedness.[67]

There are also significant differences in third-party management. BAIT already requires institutions to maintain an outsourcing register and to conduct comprehensive risk assessments in accordance with AT 9 MaRisk. In practice, this is usually implemented through contracts with IT service providers and outsourcing partners, whose risk qualification is based on materiality. DORA significantly expands this perspective: it explicitly covers all ICT services, regardless of whether they constitute formal outsourcing, and requires, in Articles 25 to 39, the maintenance of a standardized information register of all contractual relationships in the ICT context. The present register is similar to the existing outsourcing register but clearly exceeds its scope in breadth and depth, as it particularly includes the complete tracking of subcontracting chains.[68] Under DORA, the obligation to conduct risk analysis and the requirements for minimum contractual content (such as exit strategies, audit rights, and data access rules) are more strongly formalized. For LSIs, this standardization is particularly relevant in cases where previously only informal or scattered contract overviews were maintained. There is

[65] See BaFin, 2024b.

[66] See Priller, 2025, pp. 163–218.

[67] See Hellekamp, 2025, pp. 2–28.

[68] See Freßmann, et al., 2024, pp. 53–120.

also a significantly higher degree of standardization at the structural level. DORA uses uniform definitions, clear terminology, and detailed thresholds. For LSIs, this does not mean a complete system break, but it does mean a structural tightening and harmonization of requirements, which significantly increases the implementation effort both organizationally and technically. At the same time, there are significant differences in terminology, consistency, and level of detail. While BAIT deliberately uses generic terms that allow institutions room for interpretation, DORA sets out specific definitions, thresholds, and formalized processes. These range from incident reporting to risk assessment and third-party management. While this increases transparency, it also reduces flexibility and often makes adjustments to existing internal concepts unavoidable. These findings form the conceptual basis for the subsequent empirical analysis, in which the assessment of the challenges arising from DORA compared to previous BAIT practice will be specifically recorded. In addition, the expected implementation effort will be determined and potential support or adjustment needs identified.[69]

[69] See EBA, 2025, p. 7.

3 Methodology

The answers to the previously developed research questions in this study are based on a methodologically broad research design. This design enables both a structured and practice-oriented depiction of the complexity of regulatory implementation practices in LSIs. The following sections of this chapter explain the methodological approach, the operationalization of the central concepts, and the construction of the questionnaire. Subsequently, the selection of the target group, the implementation of the survey, and the specific evaluation procedure are described in detail.

3.1 Methodological Approach

To systematically examine the effects of the DORA Regulation on LSIs in the German banking sector, a deductive-quantitative research approach was chosen. This methodological combination of quantitative and qualitative components addresses the complex subject of regulatory impact and feasibility of the DORA Regulation in LSIs by collecting structurally comparable data while also allowing for contextual insights and individual assessments. The focus is on a hypothesis-driven quantitative main component, which is qualitatively supplemented by open response fields in the questionnaire and selected free-text analyses. The decision to use a quantitative approach is based on the aim to collect standardized, comparable, and statistically analyzable information that enables robust conclusions

O. Michelmann, *DORA and LSI Banks*,
https://doi.org/10.1007/978-3-658-52897-3_3

about implementation practices and the perception of regulatory challenges.[1] The focus is less on in-depth exploration of individual cases and more on the aggregated identification of trends, patterns, and key areas of strain within the LSI segment. The subject of investigation is characterized by high clarity and structure. Due to the already widely received content of the regulation in academic literature and regulatory discourse, it was possible to analytically define the central topics—particularly ICT risk management, incident reporting, resilience testing, and third-party management—in advance and to empirically operationalize them along structured categories. The derivation of research questions and hypotheses was based on a comprehensive engagement with regulatory developments, existing literature, and previous implementation experiences with comparable requirements (e.g., BAIT, MaRisk), and was both theoretically guided and practice-oriented. The study is thus based on well-founded theoretical considerations while ensuring strong practical relevance.

To implement the present design, a standardized online questionnaire was developed, representing the central data collection method of the study. The use of a questionnaire allows for efficient and systematic data collection within a heterogeneous population while maintaining comparability of responses. The questionnaire was designed along the previously defined topics and contains both closed and semi-open questions. The mixed-methods approach was chosen to capture both the breadth and depth of DORA-related burdens. The quantitative component ensures aggregation and comparability between institutions, while the qualitative component allows for an initial identification of patterns in interpretation, perceived relevance, or operational challenges. The questions were formulated to align with established regulatory terminology, thereby avoiding misunderstandings and ensuring high response validity. Elaborate qualitative individual interviews or multi-stage Delphi procedures were deliberately omitted, as these were deemed methodologically unsuitable due to the high heterogeneity of the LSI landscape and the explicitly quantitative interest in the extent of burdens. A dedicated group design with quota samples was also rejected, as achieving statistical representativeness was not a goal. Instead, the aim was to gain the broadest possible access to practical implementation experiences.

The chosen research approach consistently adheres to the scientific quality criteria of empirical research. Objectivity is ensured by a standardized survey format, which includes identical question texts, neutral scale gradations, and

[1] See Burton/Turner, 2015, pp. 1–25.

the complete omission of personal characteristics. In addition, the questionnaire was tested for comprehensibility and neutrality by independent test persons in a sample prior to the field test. Reliability is sought through the use of uniform response formats within each topic block, predominantly employing five-point Likert scales. The evaluation includes a check of internal consistency. For quantitative verification, the calculation of Cronbach's alpha for the relevant subscales is planned. To ensure content validity, the items were designed based on relevant regulatory requirements, particularly the DORA Regulation including RTS and ITS, as well as academic literature. Existing national regulations such as BAIT and MaRisk were also used as conceptual reference points to ensure compatibility with existing implementation practices. Thus, there is a close alignment between the overarching objective of the study and the content construction of the items.

The study thus pursues a hypothesis-driven, theory-based, and operationally well-defined research approach with two main objectives: On the one hand, it aims to capture the practical challenges of DORA implementation in LSIs; on the other, it seeks to make statements about the appropriateness of the proportionality principle in the European supervisory framework. The methodological approach thus enables a bridge to be built between regulatory theory and operational implementation practice, thereby making a well-founded contribution to the academic and regulatory discourse.

3.2 Operationalization and Questionnaire Construction

Based on the overarching objective of this study—to capture the main areas of strain and implementation problems of the DORA Regulation in the LSI segment—a precise operationalization of key research dimensions was carried out as part of the empirical design. In the course of the analysis, the underlying research interest was transferred into three overarching construct categories. First, the subjectively perceived implementation efforts in the relevant DORA topic areas must be considered. Furthermore, the identified implementation problems and the associated need for regulatory clarification must be taken into account. Finally, the structural comparison characteristics of the institutions, which may act as potential influencing factors on perception and burden, must also be considered. The operationalization of these constructs was based on applicable regulatory requirements, empirically proven scale formats, and relevant academic literature.

The development of individual questionnaire items was based on a multi-stage, systematically theory-driven process. The starting point of the study was the legal and regulatory derivation based on the DORA Regulation and the associated regulatory technical standards. The four central topic areas of the regulation—ICT risk management, management and reporting of ICT incidents, testing of digital operational resilience, and third-party management including the information register—were thematically structured and each transferred into scalable item groups. These groupings enable a differentiated empirical assessment of the respective drivers of burden, such as resource allocation, documentation effort, or ambiguities in the regulatory text. To specify the content dimensions and conceptual logics, key national interpretative documents were integrated into the development, particularly BAIT, MaRisk, and relevant statements from BaFin, Bundesbank, EBA, and ECB. Individual requirements that are considered potentially ambiguous by the supervisory authorities or issues that frequently appear in BaFin FAQs were translated into operational implementation components. One example is the transfer of the previous obligation for continuous classification of ICT service providers into an item formulation that specifically asks about the effort and uncertainties in the classification process. The translational logic served as an instrument for transforming normative requirements into institutionally experienced dimensions of burden. The process was supplemented by a practice-oriented refinement based on relevant professional publications. This step ensured that the relevance of the questions was not only considered from a regulatory perspective but also with regard to practical implementation within the institution. The questions were designed with particular attention to clear and non-leading wording, avoidance of redundant questions, consistent separation between closed and open questions, and ensuring a consistent response format.

In the course of the study, the standardized items, in addition to capturing structural characteristics, were used in the form of five-point Likert scales. The scales were fully verbally anchored (from "strongly disagree" to "strongly agree") and supplemented by an additional response option "no answer possible." This scaling was implemented in all main thematic blocks to ensure data comparability and reliability within the constructs. The inclusion of targeted free-text fields provided a qualitative supplement. Respondents thus had the opportunity to specify individual challenges, points of criticism, and suggestions for improvement in detail. The mixed-methods approach is also reflected at the level of the survey instruments. The use of scales allows for structured, statistically analyzable data collection. The open fields, on the other hand, enable the inclusion of context and the identification of aspects not previously anticipated.

The questionnaire was divided into several content-related and logically sequential sections. After an introduction outlining the purpose of the survey and the anonymity of data processing, the first step was to collect institution-related structural characteristics, such as total assets, number of employees, degree of digitalization, or group affiliation. These variables serve to segment the sample and analyze potential proportionality effects in regulatory enforcement. This was followed by a survey of the general perception of the DORA Regulation compared to previous national regulation (especially BAIT). The four main blocks of the questionnaire corresponded to the previously mentioned DORA topic areas and each contained questions on subjective burden as well as on comprehensibility, feasibility, and any support needs. The questionnaire concluded with open questions in which participants could describe individual challenges, identify potential relief measures, name causes of implementation challenges, or address critical points regarding regulatory design.

3.3 Target Group and Sample

The empirical study in this work aims to capture the practical challenges, main areas of strain, and implementation realities of the DORA Regulation from the perspective of German LSIs in a differentiated manner. Accordingly, the target group of the survey was defined to reflect the broadest possible spectrum of institutional practical perspectives on regulatory implementation. The survey targets professionals and managers from LSIs who are responsible in their daily work for interpreting, implementing, or monitoring regulatory requirements in the area of IT and governance. This includes, in particular, employees from the areas of information security, IT risk management, compliance, internal audit, outsourcing management, and overall bank management. The central prerequisite for belonging to the target group was knowledge of DORA implementation in the respective institution, regardless of hierarchical level or group structure. By focusing on individuals with operational or strategic responsibility, it was ensured that the assessments collected provide a well-founded evaluation of actual implementation difficulties and sources of strain from an internal institutional perspective. The explicit aim of the survey was not to generate a statistically representative sample of all LSIs in Germany, but rather to obtain high-quality feedback from individuals directly involved with DORA-related implementation issues. The methodological objective of this study is not statistical but analytical generalizability, i.e., the identification of typical patterns of strain, uncertainties, and support needs within the affected institutions. The broad thematic focus of the questionnaire on key DORA action areas and the standardized scaling of the items enable a structured capture of areas of tension regardless of the specific bank size or organizational form.

Within this overarching target group, a qualified sample was formed for the pretest and qualitative validation of the survey instrument. The selection of sample participants was targeted according to the criterion of particular professional expertise and methodological relevance. Only individuals who had already published contributions on the implementation of the DORA Regulation in relevant professional publishers or had conducted specialist seminars on the practical implementation of DORA requirements as lecturers were considered. This selection decision served to ensure an appropriate level of validity in evaluating the questionnaire prior to the field phase. Due to the close practical relevance, solid regulatory grounding, and methodological competence of the sample participants, it was ensured that feedback on comprehensibility, scaling, structuring, and content coverage of the questionnaire was based on well-founded practical knowledge. The pretest was conducted with a total of eight participants from this qualified sample. The respondents completed the questionnaire under realistic conditions and subsequently provided detailed feedback on wording logic, response options, and technical aspects of the survey. The insights and responses obtained led to targeted adjustments, including in particular the addition of an open free-text field for specifying individual causes of implementation challenges. Minor linguistic clarifications were also made to improve comprehensibility. The average completion time was considered reasonable at around 20 minutes. The version of the survey instrument resulting from the pretest forms the methodologically sound basis for the subsequent main survey.

3.4 Implementation of the Survey

The empirical survey for this study was conducted entirely online using the data protection-compliant survey tool "empirio." The technical implementation of the questionnaire took place on the platform, and participation was anonymous and voluntary via a direct link. No personal data was collected. In the introduction to the questionnaire, participants were transparently informed about the scientific purpose of the study, the expected completion time, and the basic participation conditions. In addition, there was the option to contact the author of the study via a dedicated contact address in case of questions. To maintain scientific integrity and avoid systematic bias, the invitation text explicitly stated that only one participation per institution should take place, preferably by a person knowledgeable and responsible for DORA implementation. This was intended in particular to prevent data quality from being compromised by multiple responses. The provider "empirio" also ensures that multiple participations from the same device are not possible.

The distribution of the survey link was carried out using a multi-stage, intermediary-supported procedure, with the aim of achieving the broadest possible reach within the defined target group in the LSI segment. A key aspect of the distribution strategy was the targeted approach to multipliers within relevant institutions and networks. In this context, particular mention should be made of the regional savings bank and cooperative associations, which forwarded the questionnaire to their member institutions as part of their DORA-specific working groups and specialist committees. In addition, national banking associations were contacted, which encouraged their members to participate in the survey through circulars or targeted information dissemination. Furthermore, the link to the online survey was distributed via relevant providers of practitioner seminars on IT regulation. These providers have established networks in the German LSI sector and were able to generate targeted attention through mailing campaigns and postings on professional networking sites. In addition, specialized consulting firms were involved in the study, which, as part of their mandates, maintain contacts with banks relevant to DORA. Several of these firms agreed to forward the survey to their client institutions, thereby broadening the empirical base. Based on this multi-pronged distribution strategy, a sufficient number of cases was achieved to address the central research questions of the study.

The design of the survey as a digital online questionnaire proved methodologically appropriate given the high geographical dispersion of the target group, the heterogeneous types of institutions, and the availability of potential participants in a professional context. The digital implementation enabled flexible access to the survey while reducing organizational effort and biases that can occur in telephone or face-to-face interviews. The high standardization of the implementation and the targeted selection of distribution channels resulted in a methodologically valid survey process that meets the requirements of objectivity, transparency, and target group suitability.

3.5 Data Analysis Procedure

The analysis of the collected data was based on a combined quantitative and qualitative approach, in line with the methodological standards of empirical social research. Calculations were performed using Excel, the statistical software R, and Python. The closed questions of the standardized online questionnaire were first transferred into a numerical data matrix by coding all Likert scale responses on a five-point scale (1 = "do not agree at all" to 5 = "fully agree"). The option "no answer possible" was treated as a missing value and excluded from calculations. For the four thematic blocks—ICT risk management, ICT incidents and reporting, testing digital resilience, and management of ICT third parties—means were calculated if at least half of the items were answered. The development of robust sum indices followed the specified procedure, serving as the basis for subsequent analyses.

To ensure the internal consistency of the scales, reliability was first checked using Cronbach's alpha. Values above 0.7 were considered indicative of satisfactory internal consistency.[2] All blocks showed a significantly higher level, so the aggregation of items into sum scores is considered legitimate. In addition, an exploratory factor analysis was conducted to explore the dimensional structures within the topic areas. Factorability was checked using the Kaiser-Meyer-Olkin measure (KMO) and Bartlett's test of sphericity. The number of factors was determined using the eigenvalue criterion (> 1) and the scree plot. Subsequently, a Varimax rotation was performed to ensure the interpretability of the structure.[3] This approach enables the identification of subdimensions that reveal whether the perceived burdens have content-distinct facets.

In the descriptive analysis, central tendencies and dispersions were then calculated to describe the perception of burden in the individual topic areas. In addition to means and medians, standard deviations were reported, and the items within the blocks were ranked according to the level of burden values, enabling prioritization of the main drivers of burden. On this basis, the key areas of strain were identified.

To test for systematic differences between the various groups of institutions, inferential statistical methods were used. For two-group comparisons, the Mann-Whitney U test was used, for example to differentiate between group-affiliated and non-group-affiliated institutions or between early and late starters. For comparisons with more than two groups, such as between institutions of different total asset categories or different levels of resource allocation, the Kruskal-Wallis test was used. Where the assumption of normal distribution was not violated, t-tests were also conducted, for example when comparing perceived effort between BAIT and DORA.[4] In addition, bivariate relationships between

[2] See Dennick/Tavakol, 2011, pp. 53–55.

[3] See Brown et al., 2010, pp. 1–13.

[4] See Blettner et al., 2010, pp. 343–348.

structural characteristics and burden indices were examined using Spearman rank correlations. The study not only analyzed the correlation between the degree of digitalization and perceived burden, as well as the outsourcing ratio and third-party burden, but also the relationships between the four burden blocks and between cost-benefit assessments and the burden itself.

To simultaneously consider a variety of influencing factors, a multiple linear regression analysis (Ordinary Least Squares) was also conducted. In the present study, the overall burden index was defined as the dependent variable. Independent variables included total assets, degree of digitalization, outsourcing ratio, early project initiation, and provision of additional resources. Model fit was reported using R^2 and adjusted R^2, the significance of individual predictors was tested using t-tests, and overall model significance was checked using the F-test. To ensure the assumptions of regression, multicollinearity (via variance inflation factors), normal distribution of residuals (Shapiro-Wilk), and homoscedasticity (Breusch-Pagan test) were checked.[5]

Furthermore, a cluster analysis was used to identify typical burden profiles of institutions. For this purpose, the four burden scales were standardized to ensure comparable weighting. Subsequently, a hierarchical cluster analysis using Ward's method with Euclidean distance was conducted to make an initial determination of the number of clusters. Based on the results from the dendrogram, elbow criterion, and silhouette coefficients, a three-cluster solution was determined to be optimal. A k-means cluster analysis was then performed to achieve a finer classification of the institutions.[6] In the analysis, the cluster profiles were descriptively characterized and then compared with the contextual characteristics of total assets, degree of digitalization, outsourcing ratio, resource allocation, and project start.

In addition to the quantitative methods, a qualitative content analysis according to Mayring was conducted to systematically evaluate the respondents' free-text answers. In this study, deductive categories such as documentation, reporting obligations, audit requirements, resources, third parties, and time pressure were formed. During the analysis, the categories were expanded, focusing mainly on aspects such as supervisory support, proportionality, templates, and internal coordination. Each meaningful text passage was paraphrased, coded, and finally transferred into a coding matrix. The results were presented both as a frequency

---

[5] See Socrates, 2017, pp. 1–53.

[6] See Contreras/Murtagh, 2012, pp. 1–12.

analysis and by selecting concise original quotations.[7] To ensure precise evaluation, a separate analysis was conducted for responses to questions about challenges and desired relief or clarifications.

The combination of descriptive, inferential, and multivariate methods on the one hand, and qualitative content analysis on the other, ensures a comprehensive and methodologically sound processing of the data. The methods complement each other in such a way that the research question regarding the proportionality of DORA requirements in the context of LSI banks can be answered in a differentiated and valid manner.

[7] See Janssen et al., 2016, pp. 1–13.

Results

4

The following chapter presents the central empirical findings of the online survey. The aim is to systematically prepare the perceived main areas of burden, implementation hurdles, and needs for clarification in the context of the DORA Regulation from the perspective of LSIs. The results are structured according to the thematic organization of the questionnaire and enable both a differentiated analysis of individual regulatory areas and an overarching assessment of the regulatory impact.

4.1 Analytical Evaluation of the Survey

The sample of the study comprises 49 data sets, reflecting a broad but comparatively small-LSI-dominated picture. In terms of total assets, the majority of participating institutions are in the range of 1 to 5 billion euros (n = 27). Very small institutions with less than one billion euros are represented (n = 7), but form a minority, while institutions with more than 5 billion euros also account for a substantial share (n = 15), with no institutions above 15 billion euros included. The number of employees also illustrates this typical structure: many respondents come from organizations with rather small to medium-sized workforces, while institutions with more than 1,000 employees are less frequently represented. Affiliation with a network is a defining feature, as savings banks (n = 24) and cooperative banks (n = 12) make up the overwhelming majority of the sample; only a few institutions operate outside such networks (n = 9). At the level of the surveyed organizational units, it becomes apparent that participants are distributed across different functional areas. The main focus is on IT and compliance functions, but internal audit and management are also represented, ensuring a

O. Michelmann, *DORA and LSI Banks*,
https://doi.org/10.1007/978-3-658-52897-3_4

multifaceted depiction of internal institutional perspectives. The degree of digitalization is predominantly self-assessed as average to high (MW = 3.26; SD = 0.73), while extremely low values are rare. Additionally, it is noticeable that the outsourcing share is high in most institutions (MW = 4.14; SD = 0.69), underlining the strong dependence on external ICT service providers in the LSI landscape.

The general perception of DORA requirements shows a clear pattern, which is evident in the key figures. In direct comparison to BAIT, respondents are almost unanimous in agreeing that DORA is associated with significantly higher effort (MW = 4.57; SD = 0.76). The mean is thus well above the neutral scale value of 3, and the low standard deviation indicates that this is a largely consensual assessment. The assessment of the comprehensibility of the requirements is much more heterogeneous: with a mean of MW = 2.98 (SD = 1.02), the judgments are in the neutral range, while the standard deviation points to considerable differences between institutions. While some find the requirements comprehensible, others consider them difficult to understand.

The information situation and support from the supervisory authorities are also rated only in the medium range, with a mean of MW = 3.16 (SD = 1.02). The high standard deviation signals that some institutions apparently benefit from existing publications, while others perceive the lack of clarity and late provision of guidelines as a significant burden. Regarding resources, a clearly critical picture emerges: with MW = 2.59 (SD = 0.94), the assessment is significantly below the midpoint of the scale. The majority of institutions consider their own personnel and financial resources insufficient to meet the requirements without additional effort.

The question of the meaningfulness and practical orientation of DORA is also answered in a differentiated manner (MW = 3.06; SD = 1.13). While some respondents recognize the objectives and substantive design as sensible, a considerable number perceive the requirements as formalistic or impractical. The assessment of the cost-benefit ratio is particularly striking: with MW = 4.51 (SD = 0.61), institutions almost unanimously state that the perceived effort is not commensurate with the benefit. Here, too, the low standard deviation shows that the perception of burden is almost unanimously shared. A similar picture emerges in the assessment that DORA can only be implemented by smaller institutions with considerable additional effort (MW = 4.74; SD = 0.60). In contrast, the question of whether DORA sufficiently takes into account the framework conditions of smaller institutions is answered much more critically (MW = 2.71; SD = 1.13). This confirms the perception that, although the proportionality principle is anchored on paper, it is not experienced as effective in practice. Figure 4.1 illustrates the drivers of burden

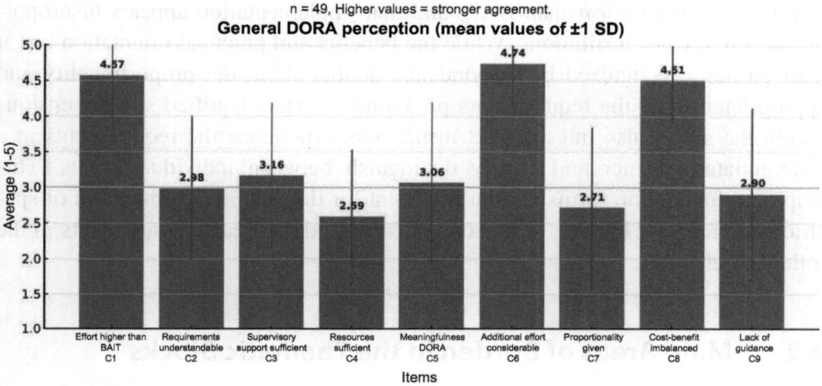

Fig. 4.1 Mean values of the general perceived DORA burdens. (Source: Own illustration)

regarding the general perception of DORA by directly comparing the mean values of the items.

The methodological foundation of the scales was ensured by reliability checks and factor analyses. In all four thematic blocks, the values for Cronbach's alpha were above 0.9 (ICT risk management: $\alpha = 0.94$; ICT incidents: $\alpha = 0.92$; resilience tests: $\alpha = 0.91$; third-party management: $\alpha = 0.96$), thus at an excellent level, so that a very high internal consistency of the items can be assumed. Aggregation into sum scales was therefore not only methodologically justified, but also forms a robust basis for further analyses. In addition, exploratory factor analyses were conducted to further examine the content structure of the blocks. For ICT risk management, a two-dimensional structure emerged with a clear separation between governance and strategy aspects on the one hand and technical and operational requirements on the other. Incident management, on the other hand, proved to be a one-dimensional construct, primarily reflecting the additional effort of reporting obligations. In testing digital resilience, two dimensions could be identified: conceptual planning and operational testing. The management of ICT third parties proved particularly complex, dividing into three sub-dimensions: contractual requirements and register obligations, control and monitoring processes, and the handling of sub-service providers including exit strategies.

The data basis is thus solid both in terms of the composition of the sample and the reliability of the measurement instruments. Furthermore, it is evident that the perception of DORA is consistently characterized by a high level of burden. Particularly striking is the almost unanimous assessment that DORA causes significantly more effort than BAIT and that implementation appears disproportionate for smaller institutions. While the benefits and practical orientation are at least partially recognized by respondents, doubts about the proportionality and appropriateness of the requirements predominate. The identified sub-dimensions within the scales also indicate that institutions experience the requirements in a differentiated manner and clearly distinguish between individual facets. This empirical foundation forms the starting point for the detailed examination of specific main areas of burden, influencing factors, and qualitative assessments in the following chapters.

4.2 Main Areas of Burden in the Thematic Blocks

The analysis of the four thematic blocks shows that institutions consistently perceive the requirements of DORA as highly burdensome, although the main areas of burden differ. In the area of ICT risk management, mean values range between 3.52 and 4.63. The burden is particularly high for the regular review, updating, and reporting of ICT risks, followed by the required transparency regarding ICT assets and their linkage to critical functions, as well as the identification of dependencies between ICT components and business processes. These values not only show a high average level of agreement but also a relatively low standard deviation, indicating broad consensus. In contrast, the transferability of existing BAIT structures to DORA requirements has the lowest burden value. The high standard deviation signals that experiences here vary widely. While some institutions can apparently draw on existing governance modules, others find adaptation difficult.

Burden peaks are even more pronounced in the area of ICT incidents and reporting obligations. The obligation to submit an initial notification within four hours is almost unanimously rated as the greatest challenge, closely followed by the coordination of initial, interim, and final reports, as well as the integration of external ICT service providers into the reporting processes. The low standard deviations for these items indicate a high level of consensus among respondents that the new deadlines and procedures create significant operational pressure. In contrast, the assessment of classification as "major" shows much greater heterogeneity. Here, perceptions diverge depending on internal interpretation or the availability of network guidelines.

Testing digital resilience is also associated with high burdens for institutions. Mean values range between 3.88 and 4.62. The highest burdens are for the requirements regarding the evaluation and documentation of tests, including action plans and repeat tests, the planning and coordination of internal and external participants, and the creation of realistic, DORA-compliant test scenarios. The comparatively low standard deviations in these areas indicate a high level of consensus. In contrast, the item on the lack of practical guidelines shows a significantly lower mean and at the same time the highest standard deviation within the block. This reflects that institutions with access to network templates or other standardized aids assess the situation much more favorably than those that rely more on in-house developments.

The management of ICT third parties is rated as the most burdensome by respondents. Mean values range between 3.71 and 4.78 and overall show the lowest standard deviation, indicating a high degree of agreement. Institutions find the creation and maintenance of a complete information register, the recording and assessment of sub-service providers along the entire value chain, and DORA-compliant contractual arrangements with aspects such as audit rights, sub-service provider chains, and exit strategies particularly burdensome. At the lower end of the burden spectrum is the assessment of whether a service provider is to be classified as "critical." Here, too, it becomes apparent that the criteria are apparently interpreted differently, depending on which network guidelines or audit standards are applied. The exposure to burden from the individual DORA dimensions is also visualized in Fig. 4.2, which contrasts the intensity of burden for the various questionnaire items.

A direct comparison of the four thematic blocks highlights the different main areas of burden. At the aggregate level, the block on third-party management is at the top with a mean of 4.55, followed by incident management, resilience tests, and risk management. The standard deviation values also confirm these findings: while the standard deviation in third-party management is 0.62, indicating particularly high consensus, it is highest in risk management at 0.83, pointing to heterogeneous experiences and varying implementation approaches.

The burden from DORA is perceived as high in all four thematic areas, but the main areas of burden differ. The burden is particularly strong and consistent in the area of third-party management, while the requirements for incident reporting are also seen as a massive challenge due to time pressure. Resilience tests and risk management are also perceived as demanding, but show greater differences in perceptions, which may be attributable to existing network solutions or already established prior experience.

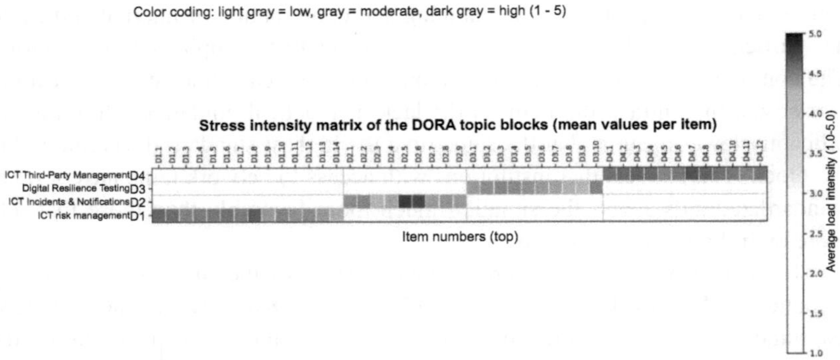

Fig. 4.2 Heatmap of burden intensity in the DORA thematic blocks. (Source: Own illustration)

4.3 Influencing Factors on the Perception of Burden

The analysis of influencing factors shows that the perception of burden from DORA cannot be explained in a one-dimensional way, but is the result of a complex interplay of institutional characteristics, resource decisions, and project strategies. Differences between institutions become apparent as soon as the data are differentiated by total assets, network affiliation, degree of digitalization, project start, resource allocation, and external consulting.

A first look at total assets shows that size alone is not a sufficient predictor of burden. The Kruskal-Wallis tests show no significant differences for three of the four thematic areas: ICT risk management ($H(2)=3.88$; $p=0.143$), incident management ($H(2)=4.11$; $p=0.128$), and third-party management ($H(2)=5.94$; $p=0.051$) are in the non-significant range. Only for resilience tests is there a significant effect ($H(2)=6.27$; $p=0.044$). Post-hoc analyses show that particularly very small institutions with total assets of less than one billion euros perceive resilience tests as significantly more burdensome than medium-sized institutions ($z=-2.46$; $p=0.043$). Thus, hypothesis H3, that smaller LSIs are overall more burdened, cannot be confirmed. However, the results suggest that in specific subareas, such as complex resilience tests, very small institutions are structurally disadvantaged.

Clearer differences emerge when comparing network and non-network institutions. Across all four thematic areas, non-network institutions show significantly higher burden values. The Mann-Whitney U tests for risk management ($U=122$;

$p = 0.018$), incident management ($U = 130$; $p = 0.030$), resilience tests ($U = 111$; $p = 0.009$), and third-party management ($U = 135$; $p = 0.036$) are all in the significant range. The mean differences are consistent: while network institutions have mean values around 4.18, non-network institutions report an average of 4.42 points. This difference shows that support through network solutions, such as templates, guidelines, or central consulting, has a noticeable relieving effect.

Another significant factor is the degree of digitalization. The comparison between institutions with high and low degrees of digitalization shows that better-digitized institutions consistently report lower burden values. This effect is particularly pronounced for resilience tests ($U = 181$; $p = 0.039$), where institutions with a high degree of digitalization have noticeably lower mean burden values. A significant difference is also seen in risk management ($U = 187$; $p = 0.047$), while incident management ($p = 0.061$) and third-party management ($p = 0.073$) are in the trend range. Correlation analyses confirm these findings: the degree of digitalization correlates significantly negatively with the burden from resilience tests ($\rho = -0.31$; $p = 0.029$) and also shows a marginally significant negative relationship in risk management ($\rho = -0.28$; $p = 0.060$). This makes it clear that technologically better-positioned institutions have an advantage, especially in complex testing procedures that can be more strongly supported digitally.

The timing of project initiation also proves to be a decisive factor. Early starters who had already begun dealing with DORA by the end of 2023 report significantly lower burdens in all thematic areas. The Mann-Whitney U tests show significant differences for risk management ($U = 188$; $p = 0.027$), incident management ($U = 192$; $p = 0.033$), resilience tests ($U = 178$; $p = 0.018$), and third-party management ($U = 200$; $p = 0.041$). Additional correlation analyses show that an early project start is negatively related to burden values ($\rho = -0.34$ to -0.41; all $p < 0.05$). Time thus proves to be a key resource: institutions that started early were able to spread out work peaks, wait for external guidelines, and leverage synergies from BAIT structures, while late starters are under massive time pressure.

A particularly clear influencing factor is also evident in the outsourcing share of institutions. The correlation analysis shows a significantly positive relationship between the intensity of outsourcing and the perceived burden in third-party management ($\rho = +0.55$; $p < 0.001$; $n = 49$). This means that the more ICT services are outsourced, the more burdensome institutions perceive the DORA requirements in this area. This relationship between increasing burden and reported outsourcing share is shown in Fig. 4.3.

A similarly clear effect is shown by resource allocation. The Kruskal-Wallis tests show significant differences between groups with no additional resources, with increased staff, with budget, and with both measures. For all four thematic

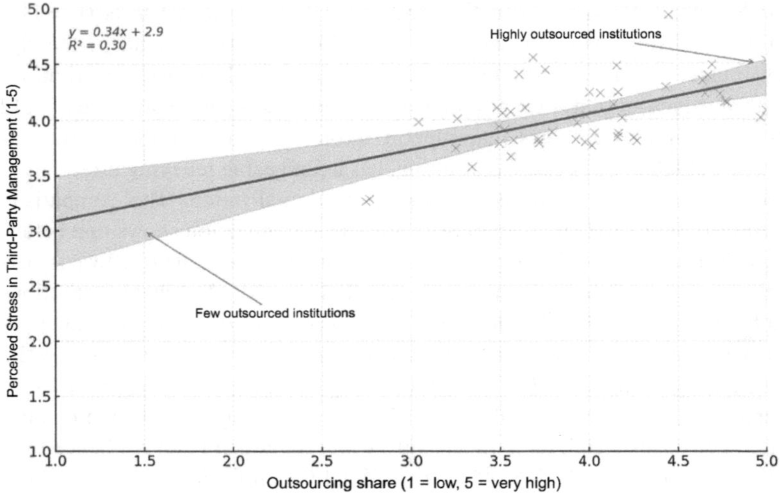

Fig. 4.3 Outsourcing share and perceived burden in third-party management. (Source: Own illustration)

areas—risk management (H(3) = 8.44; p = 0.038), incident management (H(3) = 7.95; p = 0.047), resilience tests (H(3) = 9.88; p = 0.020), and third-party management (H(3) = 10.12; p = 0.018)—the differences are significant. Post-hoc tests show that institutions with additional budget and personnel resources report significantly lower burden values than those without additional resources. These results are confirmed by correlation analyses: there are significantly negative relationships between resource allocation and perceived burden ($\rho = -0.31$ to -0.36; $p < 0.05$). Resources are thus a clear lever for relief. However, it is evident that only the combination of personnel and budget noticeably reduces the burden, while individual measures are less effective.

The role of external consulting, on the other hand, is heterogeneous. While there is a weak to moderate negative relationship for resilience tests ($\rho = -0.27$; $p = 0.048$), overall the effects are inconsistent. The Mann-Whitney U tests show no significant differences in any of the four thematic areas between institutions with and without external consulting (all $p > 0.05$). This suggests that consulting services may be helpful in specialized areas such as test design, but do not lead to systematic relief across the board.

Particularly revealing is the look at the relationships between cost-benefit assessments, the burden blocks, and their intercorrelations. The effort perceived as disproportionate correlates highly significantly with all four burden blocks ($\rho = 0.54$–0.68; $p < 0.001$). Institutions that assess the cost-benefit effect particularly critically consistently report higher burdens in all thematic areas. The four burden blocks also show strong interrelationships among themselves ($\rho = 0.69$–0.81; $p < 0.001$), indicating a general attitude of burden: those who experience high effort in one area almost inevitably perceive it in others as well.

The hypothesis testing based on the empirical results yields a differentiated picture. Hypothesis H1, that LSIs perceive the transition from BAIT to DORA as associated with higher effort, is clearly confirmed. With a mean of 4.57 (SD = 0.76), agreement is well above the neutral scale value and indicates a very strong effect. Hypothesis H2, that the greatest challenges lie in third-party management, is also confirmed: with a block mean of 4.55, this area is significantly above the other thematic areas. Hypothesis H3, that smaller LSIs are more burdened, cannot be confirmed; the burden is high across all size classes, with only very small institutions being disproportionately affected in resilience tests. Hypothesis H4, that the new reporting obligations cause the greatest operational additional effort, is confirmed in the detailed analyses: in particular, the 4-hour initial notification (MW = 4.71; SD = 0.55) and the reporting cascade (MW = 4.66; SD = 0.60) represent the peak burdens. Finally, hypothesis H5, that there is a need for regulatory clarification, is clearly supported by the qualitative analysis. Institutions primarily call for clearer requirements in the areas of documentation, reporting obligations, and audit requirements.

The perception of burden from DORA is overall strongly shaped by structural characteristics and framework conditions. While total assets alone do not provide a sufficient explanation, there are clear differences between network and non-network institutions, between early and late starters, and depending on resource allocation. Outsourcing intensity, lack of digitalization, and insufficient resources increase the burden, while network support, high digitalization, and early project planning have a relieving effect. The analysis thus provides a differentiated picture of the influencing factors, making it clear: proportionality cannot be determined solely by the size of an institution, but requires consideration of several combined determinants.

4.4 Multivariate Analyses

The descriptive and bivariate analyses conducted so far have already shown that the perceived burden on the institutions is shaped by various factors. However, to obtain a more complete picture, it is necessary to consider the simultaneous effect of multiple influencing variables. This is achieved through a multiple linear regression analysis, supplemented by a cluster analysis that reveals typical burden patterns among institutions.

In the regression model, the overall burden index, which was constructed from the four thematic blocks, was used as the dependent variable. The explanatory factors included balance sheet size categories, degree of digitalization, outsourcing share, early project initiation, and the provision of additional resources in the form of budget or personnel. The model demonstrates an overall good fit, explaining around 47 percent of the variance in perceived burden ($R^2 = 0.47$; adjusted $R^2 = 0.40$; $F(6,42) = 6.17$; $p < 0.001$). This means that a significant portion of the differences between institutions can already be explained by the selected variables. The results show very clearly that the outsourcing share exerts the greatest influence on the burden. The standardized regression coefficient is $\beta = 0.34$ ($SE = 0.07$; $t = 4.69$; $p < 0.001$). The more an institution outsources ICT services to external providers, the higher the perceived additional effort under DORA. Specifically, this means that the burden index increases on average by 0.34 points when the outsourcing share rises by one level on the five-point scale. For example, an institution moving from a medium to a high level of outsourcing experiences a significant increase in perceived burden. This finding is plausible, as institutions with extensive outsourcing must maintain comprehensive registers, adapt contracts, and monitor sub-service providers.

In contrast, the provision of additional resources has a clearly relieving effect. Institutions that were able to provide both budget and personnel for implementation report significantly lower burden values. The effect is $\beta = -0.21$ ($SE = 0.08$; $t = -2.55$; $p = 0.015$). A dual measure reduces the overall index by around 0.42 points on average. This clearly shows that targeted resource decisions are a key lever for reducing perceived burdens. The timing of project initiation also plays a role. Institutions that began implementing DORA as early as 2023 report lower perceived burdens than those that started in 2024 or later. The effect is $\beta = -0.17$ ($SE = 0.09$; $t = -1.89$; $p = 0.066$), thus marginally significant. Early starters were apparently able to better stagger tasks, leverage synergies with existing structures, and wait for supervisory guidelines before entering the critical phase of implementation. Particularly interesting is the influence of institution size. While the bivariate analyses rejected the hypothesis that smaller institutions are consistently more burdened, the regression model paints a different picture. When controlling for outsourcing, resources, and other factors, small and very small institutions report significantly higher burden values than medium-sized ones. For small institutions, the effect is $\beta = +0.29$ ($SE = 0.11$; $t = 2.61$; $p = 0.013$), and for very small institutions $\beta = +0.43$ ($SE = 0.15$; $t = 2.87$; $p = 0.007$). This finding illustrates that size differences only become clear when other contextual factors are taken into account. In other words, many larger institutions are better digitalized or better equipped, which reduces their burden. When these advantages are factored out, the structural disadvantage of smaller institutions becomes apparent. The degree of digitalization, which still showed clear effects in the bivariate analyses, loses significance in the overall model and is not statistically significant ($\beta = -0.06$; $SE = 0.05$; $t = -1.22$; $p = 0.229$). Apparently, a high degree of digitalization correlates with other relieving factors, such as better resource allocation or an early project start, so its independent effect is diminished in combination.

In addition to the regression analysis, a cluster analysis was conducted to identify typical burden profiles among institutions. Figure 4.4 illustrates the comparison of clusters A, B, and C based on the mean values of the four DORA thematic blocks.

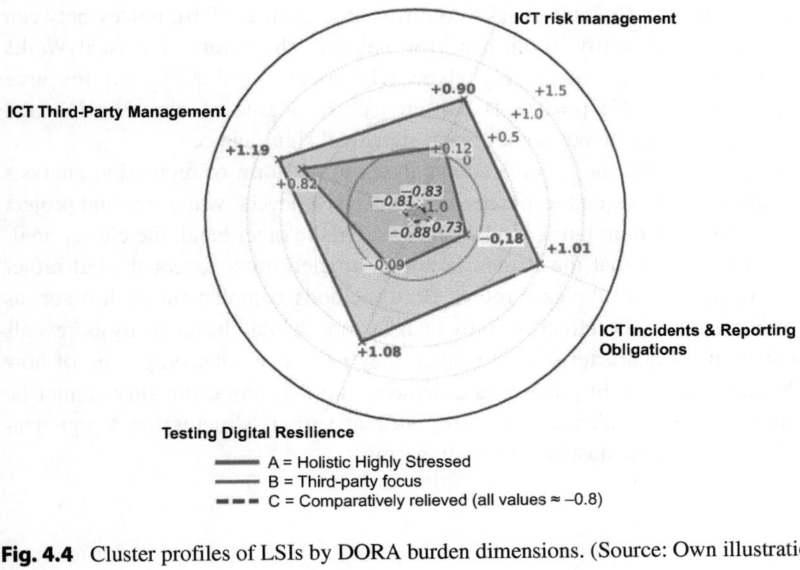

Fig. 4.4 Cluster profiles of LSIs by DORA burden dimensions. (Source: Own illustration)

The basis for this was the z-standardized values of the four thematic blocks. The result was a three-cluster solution, which proved stable both in the dendrogram and based on silhouette values (silhouette coefficient = 0.46). Cluster A comprises 20 institutions (41% of the sample) and can be characterized as "holistically highly burdened." These institutions are well above the mean in all four thematic areas (average z-values: Risk + 0.90; Incidents + 1.01; Tests + 1.08; Third-Parties + 1.19). Typically, these are small to very small institutions with a high outsourcing share, late project start, and insufficient resources. This group faces the highest risk of being overwhelmed by DORA requirements. Cluster B, consisting of 14 institutions (29%), shows a specific burden focus in third-party management (average z-value + 0.82). While the other thematic areas are at the average, the requirements for contracts, information registers, and sub-service provider management are particularly pronounced in this cluster. A characteristic feature here is that these institutions often have support from associations and started their projects early, enabling them to better cushion burdens in other areas. Finally, Cluster C comprises 15 institutions (30%) and represents the "comparatively relieved" institutions. These institutions consistently report below-average burden values (z-values: Risk –0.83; Incidents –0.73; Tests –0.88; Third-Parties –0.81). Notably, they are typically larger, highly digitalized, started implementation early, and were able to provide both budget and personnel resources. For this group, DORA implementation is evidently much more manageable. Context checks confirm these profiles. Differences between clusters are statistically significant for balance sheet total (Kruskal-Wallis $H = 8.92$; $p = 0.012$), outsourcing share ($H = 10.44$; $p = 0.005$), and resource allocation ($\chi^2 = 12.31$; $p = 0.002$). Differences in degree of digitalization and project start are visible but do not reach statistical significance.

On the one hand, the multivariate analyses in the form of regression analysis show that outsourcing and resources are the decisive levers, while size and project start are also important but secondary factors. On the other hand, the cluster analysis makes it clear that the burden is not distributed homogeneously, but rather concentrated in three typical groups. Both methods complement each other, as regression isolates the effect of individual factors, while cluster analysis reveals combinations of characteristics. Together, they provide a nuanced picture of how the burden manifests in practice and demonstrate that proportionality cannot be managed solely by balance sheet size, but that various structural and organizational characteristics must be taken into account.

4.5 Qualitative Results

The qualitative analysis of the free-text responses was conducted separately for the first two open questions. The basis was Mayring's qualitative content analysis, which combined deductive categories from the research question with inductive extensions. For each meaningful text passage, a paraphrase was created, assigned to a category, and recorded in a counting matrix. To enhance transparency, frequencies and exemplary original quotations are provided. The third open question regarding further suggestions yielded no relevant responses and was therefore not considered.

For the first open question on the central challenges ("What do you see as the main causes of the challenges in implementing the DORA requirements in your institution?"), 35 usable responses were evaluated, corresponding to a response rate of 71 percent. The most frequently mentioned issues were lack of resources (57%) and the high documentation burden (51%). The topic of supervisory support or interpretive leeway (51%) was also addressed with equal frequency, highlighting that institutions feel heavily burdened by late or unclear requirements. Other frequently cited aspects were time pressure (26%) and third-party management (23%), mainly in connection with tight deadlines and dependence on external service providers. Less frequently, but still relevant, were criticism of the lack of proportionality (17%), audit requirements (11%), and internal coordination (6%). Only one mention (3%) concerned reporting obligations, but with high practical relevance: one institution emphasized the additional workload caused by on-call duties at weekends. Quotations such as "No additional resources were provided by management" or "A lot of interpretive leeway, e.g., what exactly constitutes an ICT asset" illustrate the range of perceived problems. In summary, institutions perceive the implementation of DORA less as a technical challenge and more as a resource-related and organizational one. Particularly critical are the combination of personnel and budget shortages, extensive documentation requirements, and a lack of regulatory clarity.

The second open question focused on possible facilitations and clarifications ("What would specifically make the implementation of DORA easier for you, or where do you see a particular need for clarification?"). Here, 26 usable responses were received, corresponding to a response rate of 53 percent. Most frequently mentioned were clear and early supervisory support (42%), followed by demands for consolidated documentation (31%) and a stronger consideration of the proportionality principle (31%). In addition, 19 percent of respondents wished for concrete templates and standards that could serve as practical implementation aids.

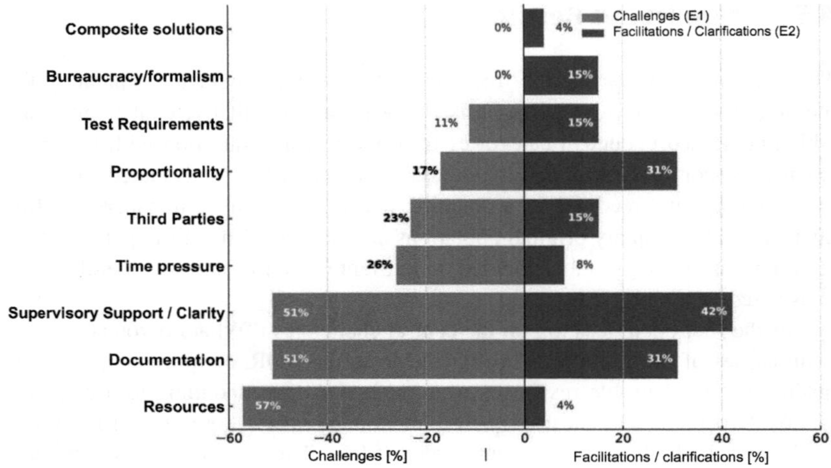

Fig. 4.5 Percentage comparison of the main qualitative categories from the free-text questions. (Source: Own illustration)

Other categories included reduction of bureaucracy (15%), clearly defined audit requirements (15%), clarifications in third-party management (15%), as well as specific suggestions such as aggregated reporting within associations (8%). Quotations such as "For implementation, it would be helpful if there were complete clarity 12 months before entry into force as to what exactly is required" or "Central provision of templates for the assessment of service providers" underscore the practical expectations of supervisors and associations. Notably, classic resource demands (4%) were mentioned only marginally. Institutions see the key to relief less in additional resources and more in better regulatory guidance.

The combination of both questions reveals a consistent picture, which is graphically depicted in Fig. 4.5.

While the challenges are mainly seen in resource shortages, documentation burden, and lack of supervisory support, the desired facilitations primarily relate to clearer and more uniform framework conditions. In other words: institutions are calling less for internal help and more for external guidance through binding guidelines, more proportionate requirements, and standardized tools. Thus, the qualitative findings complement the quantitative results by illustrating the perceived burden hotspots with concrete examples and making normative expectations of supervisors and associations visible.

Evaluation of the Findings

5

In contrast to the empirical findings that were the focus of the previous chapter, the emphasis now shifts to a systematic interpretation of these findings, the analysis of practical implementation hurdles, and the development of proportionality approaches based on these insights. As part of the analysis, the data are condensed to provide a solid foundation for drawing conclusions. Furthermore, the findings are transferred into a normative and strategic context to create a sound basis for the development of measures.

5.1 Analytical Interpretation of the Findings

The available findings reveal a clear trend that forms a consistent overall picture, in which DORA is perceived in LSI practice as a substantial additional burden compared to the previous BAIT logic. This is consistent across all four core areas: ICT risk management, incident management, resilience testing, and third-party management.[1] The significantly high agreement ratings for "increased effort" with simultaneously low variance, and the clear assessment that the effort is currently not proportionate to the benefit, indicate an almost unanimous perception. At the same time, the assessment of comprehensibility and supervisory support is heterogeneous.[2] The internal consistency of the scales is methodologically highly valid and supports the robustness of the patterns. The exploratory factor analyses do not reveal random, but rather content-wise plausibly structured subdimensions.

[1] See Sect. 4.2, pp. 43 f.

[2] See Sect. 4.5, p. 54.

O. Michelmann, *DORA and LSI Banks*,
https://doi.org/10.1007/978-3-658-52897-3_5

Thus, a "general burden attitude" can be identified, which extends beyond individual subject areas and tends to have a cross-block effect.[3]

The present study shows that the burden in the management of ICT third parties is particularly pronounced.[4] The top position of the block mean as well as the low variances for information registers, sub-service provider transparency, and contractual minimum contents demonstrate that institutions perceive these requirements as equally demanding and difficult to avoid.[5] In terms of content, there is a correspondence with the DORA-specific expansion of the scope to "all ICT services" and the formalization of register and contractual requirements that go beyond BAIT practice.[6] DORA's objective of achieving harmonization and binding requirements results in scale disadvantages for LSIs.[7] One example is the enforcement of deep, often tool-supported centralization of data and supply chain information, which were previously distributed or maintained informally. The empirical evidence shows a significant correlation between the effectiveness of the degree of outsourcing and the resulting third-party burden. This correlation confirms the underlying structural logic that a decreasing degree of in-house production is associated with an increased third-party burden.[8]

In incident management, the operational pressure is manifested in the four-hour initial notification as well as the cascade of initial, interim, and final notifications.[9] The almost unanimous agreement on the burdening effect of these requirements suggests tight time and coordination constraints, which are particularly noticeable in small institutions without 24/7 resources. The unidimensional scale structure suggests that institutions perceive the end-to-end process as an inseparable unit.[10] Partial relief will therefore only be effective if reporting criteria, reporting channels, service provider involvement, and internal escalation are addressed in a consistent overall design. The results indicate that an early project start significantly reduces the burden. This suggests that time is a critical resource for establishing new routines, readiness, and interfaces.[11]

---

[3] See Sect. 4.4, pp. 50 f.
[4] See Sect. 4.2, p. 44.
[5] See Sect. 4.2, pp. 44 f.
[6] See Sect. 4.5, pp. 53 f.
[7] See Sect. 4.3, pp. 45–48.
[8] See Sect. 4.3, pp. 47 f.
[9] See Sect. 4.2, p. 44.
[10] See Sect. 4.2, pp. 44 f.
[11] See Sect. 4.3, p. 47.

In the context of digital resilience testing, a separation of the factorial structure between conceptual planning and operational execution can be observed.[12] This division can be explained by the fact that very small institutions rate the tests as significantly more burdensome. The individuals concerned often lack both the capacity for realistic scenario design and for coordinated execution and follow-up.[13] The negative correlation between the degree of digitalization and the burden in this block supports the hypothesis that automation, integrated testing tools, and more mature process landscapes reduce the perceived load.[14] In this context, DORA acts as both a driving force and a touchstone. It establishes uniform minimum standards and makes scale advantages evident, but the absence of graduated depths and templates can lead to an overload of small-volume institutions instead of enabling a learning curve.[15]

Although ICT risk management shows the lowest level of burden in comparison, the variance is also the greatest.[16] The present analysis of the data reveals a content-related two-dimensionality, characterized by the juxtaposition of the aspects "governance & strategy" and "technical-operational effort." This two-dimensionality correlates with differences in the initial situation.[17] It was observed that institutions able to adaptively consolidate BAIT frameworks experience lower burdens. In cases where transparency regarding assets, dependencies, and reporting must be newly established, the main burden arises from documentation requirements.[18] The significant increase in the degree of formalization by DORA compared to BAIT can be identified as an explanatory factor for the observed divergence, as can the frequently expressed desire for clear guidelines and audit-proof minimum depths.[19]

The results of the comparative and correlation analyses paint a picture of a "proportionality gap" that does not run unidimensionally along the balance sheet total. The size of a company is only a significant factor in certain areas. In contrast, network support, early project initiation, additional resources, and ICT structural indicators such as digitalization and outsourcing have a much more

---

[12] See Sect. 4.4, pp. 52 f.
[13] See Sect. 4.5, p. 53.
[14] See Sect. 4.3, pp. 46 f.
[15] See Sect. 4.2, p. 45.
[16] See Sect. 4.2, p. 43.
[17] See Sect. 4.1, pp. 40 f.
[18] See Sect. 4.5, pp. 53 f.
[19] See Sect. 4.5, pp. 53 f.

robust effect. It was found that networked institutions benefit from templates, standard processes, and central interpretations, while non-network institutions face higher individual effort.[20] The effect of additional resources is described as relieving when these are translated into qualified FTEs and tools. Pure budget items without personnel effect are identified as ineffective. External consulting provides only selective benefit, especially in complex test designs. This argues for targeted, not blanket, use. The present models thus indicate a regulatory as well as pragmatic proportionality, which is oriented towards multidimensionality, focusing less on a rough size heuristic and more on the depth of outsourcing, digitalization maturity, network integration, and project lead time.[21]

The qualitative content analysis anchors these statistics in everyday experience. The three main factors are resource scarcity, documentation effort, and supervisory support perceived as late or inconsistent.[22] Desired relief measures focus on earlier, clearer guidelines, audit-proof clarifications, standardized templates, and genuine—not merely declaratory—proportionality. It is notable that demands for "more resources" are less significant in quantitative terms than structural relief levers. In areas where clear patterns, register standards, and consistency with MaRisk/BAIT are expected, bureaucracy is perceived as manageable.[23] This contrasts with structural capacity limits, which are difficult to overcome without cooperation or network solutions. These results are consistent with the previously identified burden peaks and support the hypothesis that uncertainty and fragmentation are significant factors contributing to the effort required.[24]

Translating this into the regulatory debate, it can be concluded that DORA achieves the goal of a uniform minimum standard, but in practical implementation, friction arises especially where standardization occurs without simultaneous operationalization through recognized templates, thresholds, and audit catalogues.[25] For LSIs, proportionality is less a question of lower protection objectives than of minimum process and evidence depths. Relief can be achieved if the regulation explicitly allows for supervisory-practiced graduated variants and brings these to life. The findings suggest that simplified reporting formats, modular register requirements, and network aggregations could lead to a

[20] See Sect. 4.3, p. 46.
[21] See Sect. 4.3, pp. 46 f.
[22] See Sect. 4.5, p. 53.
[23] See Sect. 4.5, p. 53.
[24] See Sect. 4.2, p. 45.
[25] See Sect. 4.5, pp. 53 f.

significant reduction in burden values.[26] Model-based estimates indicate potential scale point effects without compromising the intended resilience.[27]

5.2 Practical Implementation Hurdles

The practical hurdles to implementing DORA requirements become much more concrete along operational value chains than the pure findings might suggest. In incident management, a bundle of tightly scheduled process steps condenses into a bottleneck that is only marginally elastic: the four-hour initial notification, followed by initial, interim, and final notifications, creates a combination of 24/7 availability requirements, escalation and approval routines, and parallel root cause analysis in small institutions.[28] This constellation can only be managed in practice with a high degree of coordination. Data analysis shows that the highest burdens occur in the areas of meeting deadlines and notification sequences, as well as the integration of external ICT service providers into the reporting process. The low standard deviations in these areas indicate that these are not isolated cases, but rather a homogeneous implementation burden across institutions.[29] The variation in assessments of severity classification shows that questions of interpretation and internal guidelines influence both the effort and vulnerability to errors.[30] This suggests that time pressure and assessment uncertainty act as hurdles. The factor analysis supports this operational perception by depicting incident management as a unidimensional, inseparable construct. In everyday practice, subtasks are not isolated but experienced as an interconnected mandatory sequence, whose bottlenecks mutually reinforce each other.[31]

Testing digital operational resilience requires a combination of scenario design, cross-organizational planning, and realistic execution that has so far been unusual in many LSIs. The highest burden values are found in the evaluation and documentation of tests, as well as in the complex coordination of internal and external participants, closely followed by the creation of robust, DORA-compliant

[26] See Sect. 4.2, pp. 44 f.
[27] See Sect. 4.4, pp. 52 f.
[28] See Sect. 4.2, p. 44.
[29] See Sect. 4.2, pp. 44 f.
[30] See Sect. 4.2, pp. 44 f.
[31] See Sect. 4.5, p. 54.

test scenarios.[32] The underlying problem is not merely one of volume, but rather of structure. The empirically two-factor structure of this topic block clearly separates “test design & planning” from “execution & follow-up,” as these are two phases that require different competencies, data sets, and decision paths, and only together provide complete evidence.[33] Varying variances, for example in the absence of practical guidelines, also reflect path dependencies. Institutions with network templates and established toolchains experience less friction than those that must first establish scenarios, documentation artifacts, and evaluation logic.[34] In practice, hurdles arise, for example, when technical findings cannot be translated into audit-proof lessons-learned packages, or when external service providers must be made available for test integrations without contractual frameworks or resources to support this at short notice.[35]

In the management of ICT third parties, the discrepancy between DORA formality and LSI scale disadvantages is most evident. Creating and maintaining a complete information register requires consistent, system-supported mapping of service chains down to sub-service provider cascades. Subsequently, the assessment and documentation of subcontractors as well as DORA-compliant contractual arrangements (audit rights, sub-cascades, exit plans) must be considered. Noteworthy is the high consensus on the burden in this block, as evidenced by the low variances of the top items as well as the highest block mean in the topic comparison.[36] Even the smallest institutions are confronted with a catalogue of obligations that can only be miniaturized to a limited extent. In operational implementation, this means that contract repositories, provider inventories, and risk files often have to be consolidated from heterogeneous sources (existing contracts, service provider information, specialist registers, Excel lists) into a consistent data set, which quickly becomes a permanent construction site without centrally available reference documents. The factor-analytical division into “contract & documentation,” “management & control,” and “sub-service providers & exit strategy” also makes it clear that institutions must work simultaneously on legal, procedural, and data-logistical fronts.[37] Failures in one strand (e.g., incomplete sub-chains) undermine the evidence in another.

[32] See Sect. 4.2, pp. 44 f.

[33] See Sect. 4.4, pp. 52 f.

[34] See Sect. 4.3, pp. 46 f.

[35] See Sect. 4.5, p. 54.

[36] See Sect. 4.2, pp. 44 f.

[37] See Sect. 4.4, pp. 51 f.

In the area of ICT risk management, the hurdle profiles are less homogeneous but more differentiated. The greater variance in burden values points to highly divergent starting positions.[38] Some institutions rely on functional governance routines and BAIT-compatible documents, while others must first establish technical transparency (asset inventories, logging base, key and patch processes) and formal reporting cycles. The empirically proven dualism between "governance & strategic risk management" on the one hand and "technical implementation & operational effort" on the other manifests itself in different bottlenecks.[39] On the governance side, clarification and consistency needs predominate (strategic anchoring, risk tolerances, interfaces to emergency and exercise regimes); on the operational side, data quality and process maturity (coverage rates, up-to-dateness SLAs, tool integration) are key. The cause of failure lies less in the existence of guidelines than in the ability to translate them into robust, audit-proof templates with an appropriate creation and maintenance curve.[40]

Cross-sectional analyses identify various influencing factors whose impact on the required effort for practical implementation varies. The intensity of outsourcing is the most significant factor. As the proportion of external services increases, so do the documentation, management, and verification obligations in third-party and reporting processes.[41] This presents a dilemma, as the scale advantages originally sought through outsourcing are partially offset in the regulatory full-cost picture. In contrast, a high degree of digitalization and a very early project start prove to be robust relief factors, especially in the testing and reporting environment. This is because automation, tool stacks, and established routines smooth out peak workloads and coordination needs. Network support reduces the challenges arising from the use of templates and joint interpretation guides, while non-network institutions are more often tasked with providing greenfield services. This results in longer setup phases and increased friction at interfaces. The consistency of these patterns in both bivariate correlation analysis and the multivariate perspective is supported by the evaluation. The results provide a robust explanation for why practically identical target requirements lead to very different actual efforts.[42]

---

38 See Sect. 4.1, pp. 40 f.

39 See Sect. 4.4, p. 52.

40 See Sect. 4.5, p. 54.

41 See Sect. 4.3, pp. 47 f.

42 See Sect. 4.3, pp. 46–49.

In day-to-day implementation, difficulties arise particularly in situations where several mandatory strands compete for the same scarce resources. The issues of timely provision of reliable incident documentation by service providers and the competition between resilience tests and ICT operations for available maintenance windows, test data, and fallback plans arise in incident management and third-party management.[43] Risk management requires the same asset and process data needed for register, test, and reporting evidence. In many institutions, the fragmentation of the tool landscape exacerbates these couplings, as data cannot be transferred between CMDB, contract management, ticketing, SIEM, and reporting without media discontinuities. Finally, temporal overlaps are also of practical relevance, as the implementation of DORA projects does not take place in isolation, but coexists with alternative regulatory projects and periodic audits. This complex environment is particularly evident in institutions without dedicated, interdisciplinary DORA teams, resulting in recurring conflicts over priorities. The high, largely unanimous assessment that the effort is currently not proportionate to the benefit, as well as the strong agreement with the thesis that DORA can only be implemented in small institutions with considerable additional effort, succinctly summarize this operational experience.[44]

5.3 Potential of Regulatory Proportionality

The empirical findings suggest that the burdens arising from DORA implementation are not distributed evenly, but rather accumulate in specific bottleneck areas. In the present study, the following areas were identified as particularly critical: reporting requirements with tight deadlines and multiple layers of reporting obligations, ICT third-party management with register and contract burdens, digital resilience testing with complex scenario development, and the high documentation intensity in risk management.[45] In addition, cross-cutting issues must be considered, such as parallel regulatory obligations, ambiguous interpretative guidelines, and fragmented tool landscapes. The present results indicate that proportionality should not be conceived as a generic relief along balance sheet lines,

[43] See Sect. 4.2, pp. 44 f.

[44] See Sect. 4.5, pp. 53 f.

[45] See Sect. 4.2., pp. 45 f.

but must instead address the specific points where the burden actually arises in practice.[46]

Within the scope of the study, reporting can be considered a paradigmatic example of disproportionate burdens. According to the four-hour initial reporting requirement, a state of permanent alertness is necessary, which is labor-intensive for many institutions to achieve with their existing personnel resources.[47] Furthermore, initial, interim, and final reports must be prepared, which small teams must draft in quick succession while simultaneously conducting root cause analysis and crisis response. One way to provide relief would be to further develop the materiality matrix to give greater consideration to customer impact, criticality, and duration of the disruption. Another option for differentiating thresholds could be to introduce a reporting obligation for critical systems only after an outage of more than four hours, while for non-critical systems, only outages exceeding 24 hours would be reportable. Accordingly, minor incidents and repeat events with the same service provider could be consolidated and documented in a quarterly summary report, while serious incidents would continue to be reported ad hoc as before. In addition, standardized short reports could be implemented, containing the essential information on impact, detection, and measures in a concise template. This measure would help reduce the high number of minor reports without diluting the substantive requirements for reporting. From a proportionality perspective, it would also be advantageous to focus more on the service providers, allowing institutions to concentrate on the initial report, while providers would subsequently submit standardized detailed information in a coordinated format. This approach could close the gap in the reporting chain that was frequently criticized in the survey.[48]

The burden is even more pronounced in the management of ICT third parties than in other areas. The information register required by DORA is considered a particularly significant driver of burden, as it demands a complete and continuously updated record of all ICT services and the associated sub-service providers.[49] Smaller institutions in particular are confronted with a disproportionate effort here, as they often lack central tools, standardized templates, or the resources to track these requirements in the necessary detail.[50] A possible

---

[46] See Sect. 4.3, p. 49.

[47] See Sect. 4.5, p. 53.

[48] See Sect. 4.5, p. 54.

[49] See Sect. 4.2, pp. 44 f.

[50] See Sect. 4.3, p. 46.

approach to relief would therefore be to limit the register obligation to critical or important functions, rather than extending it to all service providers. The focus would thus be on systemically relevant services, while less significant providers would be exempt from full documentation. Another possible proportionality approach could be the introduction of a so-called trusted vendor model. In this context, the supervisory authority or a neutral body could recognize standardized assurance packages that already bundle the most important evidence. Such packages would, for example, include audited control reports, a transparent overview of sub-service provider chains, and reliable resilience metrics. For institutions, this would mean they would no longer have to compile all information themselves, but could rely on a centrally provided and audited package. Their own task would then be limited to a so-called delta analysis. This would not involve re-examining the entire service provider, but specifically identifying the differences between the standardized package and the institution's actual use. In practice, this would mean that only the services actually used, any additional risks arising from them, and any institution-specific additions or divergent contract arrangements would need to be checked and documented. This would preserve the core of individual responsibility, while significantly reducing the enormous duplication of work that currently occurs. Another proportional building block could be to focus the requirements for the information register more on a few, but verifiable, core fields and to maintain these in a digitally standardized form. Information that is needed for multiple purposes anyway could be collected using a "once-only" procedure and then reused for various verification purposes. This would strengthen consistency while avoiding redundancies. Finally, such a trusted vendor model should not only benefit network institutions, which often have access to central register solutions, but should also be equally open to non-network institutions. This could be achieved through neutral platforms or shared pools that are accessible to all LSIs under the same conditions.

In the context of digital resilience testing, relief would primarily result from standardization and tiering. The survey conducted revealed that scenario development, coordination, and documentation are perceived as particularly burdensome.[51] One possible approach could be to mandate a small number of basic scenarios to be implemented in annual rotation. For very small institutions, more in-depth tests could be scheduled at longer intervals. Between full tests, lighter exercises such as table-top formats or walkthroughs would ensure continuity. At the same time, the reuse of existing evidence should be permitted, for example

[51] See Sect. 4.2, p. 45.

when audited manufacturer reports or sectoral tests are available. This would prevent institutions from investing resources in duplicate testing. The provision of standardized playbooks with common attack scenarios by the supervisory authority could also prove particularly effective. The relief in conceptualization and the increased comparability of results would be significant advantages resulting from such implementation.

In risk management, the most significant uncertainty concerns the question of what level of detail is actually expected for documentation obligations. A difficulty faced by many institutions is deciding whether a concise, focused presentation is sufficient or whether much more extensive documentation is required.[52] This can lead to disproportionate over-documentation, tying up resources, or to an increased risk that supervisory audits will identify deficiencies because the documentation is deemed too brief. A possible proportionality approach could therefore be for the supervisory authority to specify clear minimum depths for specific core obligations. Possible examples include target coverage levels for asset inventories, up-to-date metrics for patch and vulnerability processes, or defined minimum data sets in logging. On this basis, a few clearly structured guidelines with defined measurement points could replace the previously extensive, often redundant documentation. In addition, institutions could regularly report metrics that make the quality of implementation visible, such as the rate of delayed patches, recovery times for critical systems, or the proportion of automatically recorded assets. Such an approach would align evidence more closely with objective, measurable criteria and significantly reduce interpretive leeway. On the one hand, this would avoid over-documentation; on the other, institutions would have the assurance that the evidence provided meets supervisory requirements.

Proportionate adjustments in ICT operations and change management can also lead to noticeable relief. The current basic rule is that any change to systems or applications must be documented with the same level of effort, regardless of whether it is a critical system change or merely a minor routine adjustment. For smaller institutions, this results in a particular burden, as even simple, low-risk changes must go through the same bureaucratic process as security-relevant changes to core systems. This leads to a comparatively high workload that arises independently of the quality of control and increased security. A possible solution, based on the principles of proportionality, could be the implementation of a whitelist for so-called low-risk changes. According to this list, changes could be

[52] See Sect. 4.5, p. 53.

carried out using a simplified procedure, provided specific control conditions are met. A key aspect here is ensuring the possibility of an immediate rollback at any time. Furthermore, a clear separation between development and production environments is essential. The traceability of every change must ultimately be ensured through complete logging. Under these conditions, streamlined documentation would be sufficient, while the full scope of evidence would still apply to risk-bearing system changes. Such an approach would benefit institutions by allowing the multitude of everyday routine changes to be handled with significantly less bureaucracy. The supervisory authority would ensure that full documentation and control obligations continue to apply to critical changes, so that the integrity and traceability of the process would not be compromised.

Across all topics, time emerges as a universal lever for relief.[53] The advantage of early engagement demonstrated in the survey cannot be retroactively achieved by institutions that were only able to begin implementation late, but it can be simulated through appropriate design of the supervisory framework. A central starting point would be the development of roadmaps that provide for a staggered "activation" of individual audit areas. In the first phase, the focus would be on reporting-critical processes and basic register management, while more complex requirements such as advanced resilience testing, detailed sub-service provider management, or in-depth documentation obligations would be activated in subsequent waves. Such staging would allow institutions to focus sequentially on clearly defined priorities, rather than having to achieve audit readiness in all areas simultaneously. The supervisory authority could actively support this process by publishing specific guidance documents, FAQ collections, and sample formats for each stage of the roadmap, providing institutions with reliable orientation. This would not only facilitate implementation, but also address the problem of the much-criticized uncertainty of interpretation.[54] Pilot projects, in which individual requirements are tested on a trial basis and on a smaller scale, could serve as learning platforms before they become mandatory. At the same time, a temporary restraint in supervisory audits during the first months after the regulation comes into force could effectively extend the engagement period. This would give institutions the opportunity to gain valuable months to stabilize their processes and build up audit-proof evidence, without being exposed to the immediate pressure of a formal determination. Such an approach would create an orderly rollout

[53] See Sect. 4.3, p. 47.

[54] See Sect. 4.5, pp. 53 f.

of DORA, which would both mitigate peak burdens for institutions and distribute the supervisory workload more evenly. Instead of opening all audit areas simultaneously, the supervisory authority could define priorities for staggered audits. Thematic interpretative aids could be published in parallel. For institutions, this would not only result in better planning, but also provide a practical way to compensate for the advantage of early engagement retrospectively. Precisely because time emerged from the data as one of the strongest relief factors, this form of sequencing represents a particularly effective and comparatively easy-to-implement proportionality approach that could significantly increase the practical feasibility of DORA for small and medium-sized institutions.[55]

In addition, two cross-cutting aspects are crucial for the effectiveness of proportionality. First, regulatory harmonization is required to avoid multiple reporting and conflicting obligations.[56] Consistent integration of DORA and, for example, the existing outsourcing management guidelines would provide a noticeable relief effect for LSIs. In the long term, banking supervisory reporting could be converted to a unified data model such as BiRD/iReF, which would establish a "once-only" logic. Second, differentiation by institution size is necessary.[57] Small and very small institutions should have their own relief category, which reduces frequencies, streamlines documentation requirements, and allows standard processes at longer intervals. It would also make sense to differentiate further within the group of LSIs. Small institutions would continue to fulfill all core obligations, but in reduced depth or at lower frequency, for example through simplified reporting formats, annual instead of semi-annual reports, or reduced documentation scope. For very small institutions, a minimum requirements logic could apply, focusing obligations on a manageable set of core requirements. Necessary measures would include, in particular, a simplified register with a reduced number of verifiable fields, an annual risk review based on defined metrics, and basic operational resilience exercises. The latter should not be conducted annually, but at intervals of about three years. Such staging would specifically close the proportionality gap identified in the survey, as it is based not on balance sheet size, but on actual organizational capacity.

---

[55] See Sect. 4.3, p. 47.

[56] See Sect. 4.5, pp. 53 f.

[57] See Sect. 4.5, p. 53.

Finally, the unequal starting position between network and non-network institutions remains a central issue.[58] While network institutions benefit from shared templates, joint registers, and standardized audit paths, private banks report a significantly higher workload. This inequality cannot be fully compensated without devaluing the benefits of the network. Nevertheless, neutral platforms or industry pools could ensure that non-network institutions also have access to standardized assurance packages, audits, and templates.

5.4 Strategic Implications

The proportionality approaches developed in Sect. 5.3 show that achieving proportionality in the context of DORA is not automatic, but rather a principle that must be consciously managed and firmly anchored in the regulatory architecture in order to be effective. The strategic challenge lies in understanding the proportionality mechanisms derived from the study not as isolated relief measures, but as a starting point for a fundamental realignment of supervisory control. The findings of this study suggest that regulatory burdens do not arise by chance, but result from systemic structures, particularly unclear expectations, redundant reporting obligations, and a lack of temporal staging in implementation.[59] Supervisors should interpret these insights as strategic guidelines and deliberately transform them into permanent management instruments. The goal is to create a regulatory framework in which proportionality is not merely a subsequent corrective, but functions as an integral part of regulatory design from the outset.

A central strategic implication concerns the issue of expectation transparency. The empirical results of the study suggest that the prevailing uncertainty regarding the required level of evidence is a key factor in over-documentation and the resulting inefficiency.[60] From a strategic perspective, it is therefore essential that supervisors move from principle-based to more calibrated expectation systems. In this context, it is crucial that minimum depths, core metrics, and types of evidence are standardized. Standardization increases legal certainty for LSIs and simultaneously relieves supervisors, as audits are based on transparent and comparable criteria. This achieves an institutional operationalization of proportionality, reducing dependence on individual examiner interpretations. Furthermore, the

---

[58] See Sect. 4.3, p. 46.

[59] See Sect. 4.5, p. 53.

[60] See Sect. 4.5, pp. 53 f.

identified burden hotspots, particularly in reporting and ICT third-party management, highlight the strategic necessity of embedding regulatory simplification as a structural objective.[61] The materiality logic concept and the "once-only" principle developed in this study should therefore serve not only as case-by-case solutions, but as fundamental principles of future regulation. According to the premise of proportionality, a harmonized supervisory approach emerges that systematically reduces redundancies between DORA, NIS2, CRA, and MaRisk, and focuses on actual risk exposure rather than formal completeness. Such integration requires more data-driven and digital management of supervisory and reporting processes to optimize information flows between authorities and institutions.

The time component highlighted in the study is also of considerable strategic importance.[62] The empirically proven advantage of early engagement can be used by supervisors to generally sequence the introduction of new regulations over time. Instead of simultaneous activation of all obligations, a gradual implementation under clearly defined roadmaps is recommended, providing institutions with predictable transition periods. From a strategic perspective, this implies a departure from the "big bang" principle of regulatory introduction in favor of an iterative model that enables learning and adaptation. Such mechanisms not only contribute to more stable implementation quality, but also foster trust in a predictable supervisory practice. Another area of strategic implication arises from the heterogeneity within the LSI landscape demonstrated in this study.[63] Supervisors should not only record this institutional diversity statistically in the future, but use it as a basis for differentiated supervisory intensity. The tiering between small and very small institutions proposed in this study could serve as a blueprint for a systematic division of supervisory segments. Accordingly, proportionality would no longer be realized ad hoc through discretionary leeway, but through formalized categories based on risk profile, complexity, and resource situation.

Finally, the empirical results allow strategic conclusions to be drawn for the European supervisory level.[64] The challenges identified in this study, such as multiple regulation, lack of interpretative guidance, and inconsistent audit practices, result from a lack of alignment between European and national requirements. In the long term, proportionality should therefore not be understood as a national

[61] See Sect. 4.2, p. 45.
[62] See Sect. 4.3, p. 47.
[63] See Sect. 4.1, pp. 40 f.
[64] See Sect. 4.5, p. 54.

fine-tuning instrument, but as a common European management logic. Supervisory authorities such as the EBA, ESMA, and EIOPA should further develop the flexibilities embedded in DORA institutionally and promote uniform application in the member states through technical standards and guidelines. This would ensure that proportionality does not remain a German special path, but becomes a core element of a European supervisory culture.

Proportionality should thus not be understood as a means of deregulation, but as a strategic management instrument of modern supervision in a uniquely evolved national banking system. It enables differentiated application of the same rules to heterogeneous institutions, ensures resource focus, and simultaneously improves supervisory quality. For this effect to materialize, however, supervisors must actively shape it through clear expectation definitions, tiered audit mechanisms, harmonized rulebooks, and shared platforms. In view of the statement by Mark Branson quoted at the beginning of this study and recent developments in the context of supervisory proportionality communications, the developments towards anchoring proportionality as a strategic guiding principle of German supervisory practice are taking ever more concrete shape. In such a framework shaped by the idea of proportionality, DORA too can truly achieve its intended balance between digital resilience and regulatory feasibility.

Conclusion and Outlook 6

The concluding chapter of this work summarizes the central findings of the study, situates them within the academic discourse on proportionality in banking supervision, and derives practical as well as supervisory policy recommendations. It reflects on the insights gained in light of the research questions and highlights the implications for the future design of the regulatory framework.

6.1 Key Findings

The study demonstrates that the implementation of DORA presents significant practical challenges for LSIs. The majority of surveyed institutions view the regulation as a considerable additional burden compared to existing frameworks, particularly BAIT. The perceived burden arises less from the protection objectives themselves and more from the specific design of the implementation, characterized by short deadlines, extensive documentation requirements, complex proofs, and unclear expectations regarding the required depth. While the goal of strengthened digital resilience is generally shared, many institutions perceive an imbalance between effort and benefit.

The burden is concentrated in three key areas: the management of ICT third parties, reporting requirements, and testing of digital resilience. The information register stands out as a primary driver, as the ongoing recording and assessment of all service providers and sub-service providers is organizationally unmanageable for many smaller institutions. In reporting, the four-hour initial notification and multi-stage reporting obligations lead to a state of permanent alert, while the involvement of external service providers often fails due to practical limitations.

O. Michelmann, *DORA and LSI Banks*,
https://doi.org/10.1007/978-3-658-52897-3_6

In the area of resilience testing, scenario development, test execution, and follow-up are perceived as particularly resource-intensive.[1]

There are clear structural differences between the institutions.[2] The burden depends less on the total assets and more on organizational conditions: outsourcing intensity, group support, degree of digitalization, and timing of project initiation are decisive factors. Institutions that engaged early or had access to group solutions report significantly lower burdens, while independent institutions suffer more from the internal workload. Thus, the variance is explained less by size and more by differing starting conditions and support structures.[3]

Overall, the study confirms a clear proportionality gap. While DORA aims for a uniform level of resilience, its high level of detail creates a regulatory intensity that disproportionately affects smaller institutions. Unclear audit depths and redundant documentation requirements often mean that formal proofs overshadow the actual resilience gains. The findings underscore the need for clear expectations, graduated requirements, and a consistent operationalization of the proportionality principle within the DORA framework.

6.2 Academic Contextualization

This work makes a scholarly contribution to the discussion on proportionality in banking supervision by empirically applying this principle to the field of ICT-related regulation for the first time. Although proportionality has already been discussed in the context of capital requirements, reporting, or governance structures, there has been little research systematically applying this supervisory principle to the requirements of digital resilience. However, the DORA regulation creates a new regulatory field in which questions of appropriateness and feasibility are particularly pressing. This work addresses a central academic gap by no longer viewing proportionality solely as a legal or political guiding principle, but as an empirically measurable variable that can be analyzed and evaluated based on concrete burden drivers. The study thus operates at the intersection of regulatory economics, supervisory research, and organizational research. In this context, proportionality is understood as a dynamic balance between regulatory stringency and operational feasibility. The academic value lies in demonstrating how this

[1] See Sect. 4.2, pp. 44 f.
[2] See Sect. 4.3, pp. 50 f.
[3] See Sect. 4.3, pp. 52 f.

balance can be empirically determined. This is not based on normative assumptions, but on the measurable impact of regulation on the structures, processes, and resources of supervised institutions. In this context, the proportionality principle evolves from an abstract formula to a verifiable management tool. As a result, the regulatory burden is made verifiable both quantitatively and qualitatively.

Finally, the work expands the academic discourse on the regulation of digital systems in the financial sector by interpreting proportionality as a constitutive element of future-proof supervisory practice. In times of increasing technologization and regulatory density, it provides arguments that stability and resilience are achieved not through maximum detail, but through smart differentiation. The findings suggest that standardization, reliance principles, and clarity regarding expectations are key levers for effective and proportionate regulation. The work thus positions itself at the interface between academia and practice and provides an empirically grounded basis on which future research and policy decisions on the further development of proportionality in the digital regulatory framework can build.

6.3 Recommendations for Action

The findings show that the effectiveness of DORA depends largely on the extent to which the supervisory authority concretizes and operationalizes the legal framework. The aim is not to relax requirements, but to achieve intelligent regulation that combines the same protection objectives with greater feasibility and less friction.

A key area for action concerns clarifying expectations and audit depths. A significant part of the burden does not stem from the regulation itself, but from uncertainties about the scope and depth of evidence required. Supervisors should therefore define bindingly which key figures, documentation standards, and audit depths are considered sufficient. In addition, standardized templates and interpretative aids should be provided to avoid redundant proofs and foster a common understanding between supervisors, auditors, and institutions. Equally important is a structured timeline for implementation. DORA requires the introduction of numerous processes that can only be realized in stages. A supervisory roadmap with prioritized topics and accompanying guidance documents would mitigate peak burdens, promote learning curves, and enable supervisors to provide targeted quality support.

Furthermore, supervisors should actively contribute to harmonizing the regulatory landscape. Overlaps between DORA, NIS2, CRA, and MaRisk increase complexity and workload. Uniform terminology, coordinated reporting obligations, and the principle of once-only data collection could provide significant relief. The introduction of digital interfaces and standardized data models would further help automate reporting processes and avoid redundancies. Another lever lies in the management of ICT third parties. Trusted vendor models or central register pools could bundle verified proofs for frequently used service providers. Institutions could then use certified assurance packages and focus on institution-specific audits—a strategy that would notably relieve smaller institutions while simultaneously improving the data quality available to supervisors.

Finally, proportionality should also be institutionally anchored. In addition to differentiation by complexity and risk profile, graduated relief categories for small and very small institutions should be defined. These could include lower audit frequencies, simplified documentation requirements, and reduced reporting obligations to achieve regulatory objectives with a reasonable level of effort.

6.4 Methodological Limitations

The explanatory power of this study is subject to several methodological limitations that must be considered when interpreting the results. These constraints reflect typical challenges of empirical research methods. For example, the survey was designed as a cross-sectional, standardized online questionnaire, without experimental or longitudinal elements. The observed relationships, such as the relieving effect of an early project start, can therefore only be interpreted as associations, not as causal effects. Likewise, unobserved influencing factors, such as an institution's organizational maturity or pre-existing digitalization initiatives, cannot be fully ruled out. The study is thus suitable for deriving directional statements and identifying patterns, but not for establishing clear cause-and-effect relationships.

The sample is also subject to certain limitations, as it comprises 49 participating institutions, providing a differentiated picture of the German LSI landscape, but is not probabilistically drawn and does not include larger LSI institutions. Recruitment via associations and professional networks may lead to participant selection, as particularly burdened or well-organized institutions may be more likely to participate. Nevertheless, the generalizability of the results to German LSIs can be considered good overall due to the composition of the national banking landscape, whereas transferability to other European jurisdictions is only limited.

At the measurement level, further methodological limitations arise. The analysis relies on self-reports using standardized Likert scales. Metric treatment was applied, although strictly speaking these are ordinal data. While this practice is widespread, it can lead to slight distortions if the intervals between response categories are not perceived as equal. Furthermore, the use of mean indices may smooth out or exaggerate dependencies between individual items. High reliability values indicate internal consistency, but may also reflect redundancies in the scale structure.

The exploratory factor analyses and cluster procedures used to structure the data are also model-building and highly sample-dependent. With a limited number of cases, there is a risk that minor changes in the data or starting values may lead to slightly different factor solutions. The identified typology of institutional groups (holistically highly burdened, third-party focus, relieved) should therefore be understood as a heuristic structural proposal rather than a definitive classification. The regression model, with an explanatory power of around 47 percent, is substantial but not exhaustive. Possible unobserved variables, such as experience with IT audits or specific governance characteristics, may remain unaccounted for. Common-method bias may also become a significant influencing factor in this study. Since key variables such as burden, resource situation, or degree of digitalization were collected using the same instrument and at the same time, common method variance may partially reinforce the observed relationships. As objective data, such as actual project budgets or hours spent, were not available, validation using external indicators was not possible. The results are therefore based on the subjective perceptions of respondents, which are nonetheless considered a valid source for assessments and trend analyses, but should not be confused with hard performance data.

It should also be noted that the qualitative component of the study has certain limitations. The analysis of open text fields provides valuable contextual additions, but is based on a selective subset of participants. It is likely that individuals with strong opinions or extensive experience were particularly inclined to share their perspectives, which may result in certain positions being overrepresented. In addition, no formal intercoder reliability was established, so potential bias from subjective interpretations cannot be ruled out. Finally, it should be considered that data collection took place in an early phase of DORA regulation. The results therefore reflect a current state that may be modified by increasing precision and greater implementation experience among institutions. The present assessments of burden and proportionality thus reflect the transition from the planning to the implementation phase, but not the long-term stabilized state.

Despite these limitations, extensive quality assurance measures were implemented, including reliability analyses, plausibility checks, non-parametric tests, and triangulation of quantitative and qualitative findings. These steps contribute to increasing the internal validity of the results, but cannot fully compensate for the structural limitations of the research design. The results should therefore be interpreted as robust directional statements that reveal clear patterns and relationships, but do not provide precise parameters for the entire population. This study can thus be regarded as an empirically grounded compass that provides valuable insights into the burden structure and proportionality gaps within the DORA framework.

6.5 Further Research Approaches

As DORA represents a novel and dynamic regulation, academic engagement with its practical effects is only just beginning. This study provides an initial empirical approach to the burden structures and proportionality gaps among LSIs. However, it can only be seen as a starting point for a more systematic research agenda that more closely integrates quantitative, qualitative, and regulatory dimensions. A central focus of future research initiatives should be on replicating and scaling the study. A larger and more heterogeneous sample, including systemically important institutions (SIs), specialist banks, and foreign jurisdictions, could significantly increase the generalizability of the findings. In particular, a comparative analysis of LSIs and SIs is needed to determine whether the perceived differences in burden are primarily due to size and complexity factors.

In addition, a longitudinal design would be of particular academic value. An empirical study in the form of a before-and-after analysis, covering the period before entry into force and after full implementation, could capture changes in burden levels, resource requirements, and perceptions of proportionality over time. The effectiveness of the identified proportionality measures, such as roadmaps or trusted vendor models, could be evaluated directly. This study concludes that impact studies are a suitable means of determining whether supervisory relief measures lead to measurable reductions in burden without jeopardizing the objective of digital resilience. Furthermore, there are also numerous methodological developments to be made. A confirmatory factor analysis or structural equation models could empirically validate the scales developed exploratively in this work and test whether a generalizable burden factor can be identified. In addition, the development of a multi-criteria score for operationalizing proportionality would be useful, integrating dimensions such as outsourcing intensity, resource availability, degree of digitalization, and project initiation. Such a score could serve as a management tool in the long term to better align regulatory requirements with the capabilities of individual institutions. Quasi-experimental designs, such as difference-in-differences analyses for staggered implementation or instrumental variable approaches for advisory intensity and resource allocation, could also provide causally robust evidence on the mechanisms of regulatory relief. Alongside these quantitative deep dives, expanding qualitative research is also advisable. Mixed-methods approaches, including case studies on group structures, shared service models, or governance processes for ICT third parties, could help develop a deeper understanding of how proportionality is actually practiced in organizational settings.

Process-tracing analyses within individual institutions or groups could also reveal which internal factors promote or hinder the implementation of relief mechanisms. This would allow a link to be established between quantitative burden indices and the practical reality of institutional management. In addition, future studies should further test the robustness and stability of previous findings. Multiple imputation for missing values, bootstrapping, alternative clustering approaches, or weighting by institutional characteristics could potentially help minimize distortions and increase the methodological robustness of the results. Furthermore, testing for measurement invariance between different groups, such as between group-affiliated and non-group institutions or between size classes, would be necessary to ensure that the scales used function equally across all groups and thus allow for comparable statements.

Finally, this gives rise to a long-term research question at the conceptual level. The question arises as to how proportionality can be permanently anchored in future regulatory waves without undermining the objective of resilience. An in-depth analysis of the role of European supervisory authorities is required, particularly with regard to their ability to operationalize proportionality through guidelines, standards, and consultation processes. In addition, the interfaces between DORA and regulations such as NIS2 or MaRisk offer scope for further research. The aim of this research is to identify harmonization potential and empirically measure regulatory coherence. This work thus provides an initial empirical approach to DORA and proportionality, while a deeper academic exploration is still pending. Future studies should therefore combine broader data bases, differentiated methods, and interdisciplinary perspectives to sustainably investigate the viability, impact, and institutional integration of proportionality in European ICT supervision.

References

Aben, Janika/Etti, Paula (2023): European Digital Finance, in: Hamulak, Ondrej/Kerikmäe, Tanel/Troitino, David (Eds.), Digital Development of the European Union—An Interdisciplinary Perspective, Cham, pp. 67–84.

AFM (Niederländische Finanzmarktaufsicht) (2024): Getting ready for DORA: Testing of the digital operational resilience, in: AFM Supervision DORA Update, Vol. 5, pp. 1–8.

Alugoju, Narasimha (2024): Digital Operational Resilience Act (DORA), in: International Journal of Computer Engineering and Technology, Vol. 15, No. 6, pp. 911–921.

Ananieva, Yuliia/Zhytar, Maksym (2025): Methodological justification of state regulation and self-regulation of the development of the banking sector and its financial security, in: Financial and Credit System: Prospects for Development, Vol. 3, No. 18, pp. 20–34.

Arnaoudova, Kristina/Nisheva-Pavlova, Maria (2023): Enterprise data and semantic modelling: conceptual model of information technology incident management, in: Annual of Sofia University St Kliment Ohridski Faculty of Mathematics and Informatics, Vol. 110, pp. 25–36

Avsuvarova, Khanim (2023): Navigating Digital Transformation: Unpacking the Impact of DORA on the Insurance Landscape, o.O.

Barg, Maximilian/Stargardt, Helene (2025): DORA-Umsetzung—Die größten Herausforderungen im Detail, in: FLF-Sonderdruck, Vol. 2, pp. 1–5.

Bauer, Stefan (2023): Digital Operational Resilience Act (DORA): Wie hoch wird die nächste Welle der Regulierung?, in: DataNavigator, Vol. 20, pp. 1–6.

Begozzi, Valerio/Oldani, Matteo/Terizzano, Francesca (2023): The growing importance of digital risk & governance, in: Risk Management Magazine, Vol. 18, No. 2, pp. 27–36.

Benroider, Edward/Elshuber, Christoph/Neumannova, Anita (2023): The Digital Operational Resilience Act for Financial Services: A Comparative Gap Analysis and Literature Review, in: Christodoulou, Klitos/da Cunha, Paulo/Papadaki, Maria/Themistocleous, Marinos (Eds.), Information Systems—19th European, Mediterranean, and Middle Eastern Conference, EMCIS 2022 Proceedings, pp. 570–585.

Bernnat, Rainer/Pötsch, Jordan (2025): Regulierung von Künstlicher Intelligenz in der EU—Praxisbezogene Lösungsansätze für die Sicherheit von KI-Anwendungen, Wiesbaden, pp. 197–215.

O. Michelmann, *DORA and LSI Banks*,
https://doi.org/10.1007/978-3-658-52897-3

Biernat, Holger/Maksimovic, Tomislav (2019): Bankaufsichtliche Anforderungen an die IT (BAIT)—Konzepte zur Implementierung der neuen Vorgaben, Wiesbaden, pp. 93–188.

Blettner, Maria/du Prel, Jean-Baptist/Hommel, Gerhard/Röhrig, Bernd (2010): Auswahl statistischer Testverfahren, in: Deutsches Ärzteblatt, Jg. 107, Heft 19, pp. 343–348.

Blix, Fredrik/Popov, Oliver/Seid, Elias (2025): Cyber Resilience Using ASFA: DORA-Compliant Threat-Led Penetration Testing, in: Faramondi, Luca/Hämmerli, Bernhard/Oliva, Gabriele/Panzieri, Stefano/Pascucci, Federica (Eds.), Critical Information Infrastructures Security—19th International Conference, CRITIS 2024, Revised Selected Papers, Rom, pp. 269–288.

Boggini, Clara (2024): Reporting cybersecurity to stakeholders: A review of CSRD and the EU cyber legal framework, in: Computer Law & Security Review, Vol. 53, pp. 1–8.

Bornemann, Kerstin/Brandes, Felix (2017): Rechtlicher Rahmen des Digital Banking, in: Brühl, Volker/Dorschel, Joachim (Eds.), Praxishandbuch Digital Banking, Wiesbaden, pp. 357–406.

Boss, Michael/Lederer, Gerald/Mujic, Nadja/Schwaiger, Markus (2018): Proportionality in banking regulation, in: Monetary Policy &the economy, Vol. Q2/18, pp. 51–70.

Branson, Mark (2024): Jahrespressekonferenz 2024—Rede von Mark Branson, Präsident der BaFin: https://www.bafin.de/SharedDocs/Veroeffentlichungen/DE/Reden/re_220503_jahrespressekonferenz2024.html, *zuletzt abgerufen am 08.10.2025.*

Brown, Ted/Onsman, Andrys/Williams, Brett (2010): Exploratory Factor Analysis: A Five-Step Guide for Novices, in: Paramedicine, Vol. 8, pp. 1–13.

Buchmüller, Patrik/Puntus, Georg/Tuder, Georg (2019): Regulatorische Agenda im ersten Halbjahr 2019: Wesentliche Neuerungen und Umsetzungsprioritäten für deutsche und österreichische Banken, in: Zeitschrift für Finanzregulierung und Finanzinstitutionen (ZFF), Vol. 1, pp. 5–25.

Bundesanstalt für Finanzdienstleistungsaufsicht (2024a): Aufsichtsmitteilung: Kleine und sehr kleine Kreditinstitute—Proportionalität in den Anforderungen der BaFin an das Risikomanagement, Fassung vom 26.11.2024.

Bundesanstalt für Finanzdienstleistungsaufsicht (2024b): Bankaufsichtliche Anforderungen an die IT (BAIT)—Rundschreiben 10/2017 (BA), Fassung vom 16.12.2024.

Burton, Richard/Turner, Scott (2015): Research Design for Mixed Methods: A Triangulation-based Framework and Roadmap, in: Organizational Research Methods, Vol. 20, No.2, pp. 1–25.

Busch, Dany (2024): The Future of Equivalence in the EU Financial Sector, in: European Business Organization Law Review, Vol. 25, pp. 3–23.

Buttgieg, Christopher/Zimmermann, Beatriz (2024): The digital operational resilience act: challenges and some reflections on the adequacy of Europe's architecture for financial supervision, in: ERA Forum, Vol. 25, pp. 11–28.

Camacho, Elena/Donnelly, Shawn/Heidbrecht, Sebastian (2024): Digital sovereignty as control: the regulation of digital finance in the European Union, in: Journal of European Public Policy, Vol. 31, No. 8, pp. 2226–2249.

Carrillo, Elena (2024): Cybersecurity in European Financial Institutions: New Grounds for Corporate Governance Reform, in: European Business Law Review, Vol. 34, No. 7, pp. 1133–1166.

Chiarella, Carlo/Cuadros-Solas, Pedro/Rossi, Ludovico (2025): Supranational Supervision and Bank Governance, Madrid.

Clausmeier, Dirk (2023): Regulation of the European Parliament and the Council on digital operational resilience for the financial sector (DORA), in: International Cybersecurity Law Review, Vol. 4, pp. 79–90.

Contreras, Pedro/Murtagh, Fionn (2012): Algorithms for hierarchical clustering: An overview, in: Wiley Interdisciplinary Reviews: Data Mining and Knowledge Discovery, Vol. 00, pp. 1–12.

Correia, Ancleto/Goncalves, Antonio (2024): Regulatory Convergence and Divergence: A Study on the Synergies and Conflicts among Key Cybersecurity European Legslation, in: The 16th Mediterranean Conference on Information Systems (MCIS) and the 24th Conference of the Portuguese Association for Information Systems (CAPSI), Porto, pp. 1–20.

Dennick, Reg/Tavakol, Mohsen (2011): Making sense of Cronbach's alpha, in: International Journal of Medical Education, Vol. 2, pp. 53–55.

Duggan, Derek (2024): The impact of the Digital Operational Resilience Act on financial market infrastructures in Europe, in: Journal of Securities Operations & Custody, Vol. 16, No. 4, pp. 344–350.

Europäische Kommission (2024a): Delegierte Verordnung (EU) 2024/1772 der Kommission vom 13. März 2024 zur Ergänzung der Verordnung (EU) 2022/2554 des Europäischen Parlaments und des Rates durch technische Regulierungsstandards zur Festlegung der Kriterien für die Klassifizierung von IKT-bezogenen Vorfällen und Cyberbedrohungen, der Wesentlichkeitsschwellen und der Einzelheiten von Meldungen schwerwiegender Vorfälle, in: Amtsblatt der Europäischen Union, L 2024/1772 vom 25. Juni 2024.

Europäische Kommission (2024b): Delegierte Verordnung (EU) 2024/1773 der Kommission vom 13. März 2024 zur Ergänzung der Verordnung (EU) 2022/2554 des Europäischen Parlaments und des Rates durch technische Regulierungsstandards zur Spezifizierung des detaillierten Inhalts der Leitlinie für vertragliche Vereinbarungen über die Nutzung von IKT-Dienstleistungen zur Unterstützung kritischer oder wichtiger Funktionen, die von IKT-Drittdienstleistern bereitgestellt werden. Amtsblatt der Europäischen Union, L 2024/1773 vom 25. Juni 2024.

Europäische Union (2022): Verordnung (EU) 2022/2554 des Europäischen Parlaments und des Rates vom 14. Dezember 2022 über die digitale operationelle Resilienz des Finanzsektors und zur Änderung der Verordnungen (EG) Nr. 1060/2009, (EU) Nr. 648/2012, (EU) Nr. 600/2014 sowie (EU) Nr. 909/2014. Amtsblatt der Europäischen Union, L 333 vom 27. Dezember 2022.

European Banking Authority (2024): Draft Regulatory Technical Standards on ICT Risk Management Frameworks pursuant to Article 15 of the Digital Operational Resilience Act (DORA).

European Banking Authority (2025): Final Report—Guidelines amending Guidelines EBA/GL/2019/04 on ICT and security risk management (EBA/GL/2025/02, 11/02/2025).

Fernandes, Joao/Ignaim, Karam (2024): Improving Incident Management Processes with Feature Models, in: Journal of Cyber Security and Mobility, Vol. 13, No. 4, pp. 701–724.

Finanzmarktaufsicht Österreich (FMA) (2025): IKT-Risikomanagement unter DORA—Erfahrungen aus der Aufsichtspraxis, in: FMA—Reden wir über Aufsicht, Vol. 5, pp. 1–4.

Frantz, Christopher/Kianpour, Mazaher (2024): Analysis of Institutional Design of European Union Cyber Incident and Crisis Management as a Complex Public Good, in: Regulation & Governance, Vol. 1, pp. 1–26.

Freßmann, Andreas/Ostendorf, Ralf/Smeets, Mario (2024): Robotic Process Automation in Use—Strategic Orientation, Practical Implementation, Audit-Proof Implementation, Wiesbaden, pp. 53–120.

Gauthier-Maxence, Celine (2024): European Cybersecurity and AI Framework: Towards Proactive Regulation for a Secure Digital Future, in: EU Law Live, Vol. 212, pp. 1–8.

Giannino, Antonio/Sertori, Federico/Valenti, Francesca (2023): Is DORA the dawn of a new era for cybersecurity compliance in the EU's financial sector?, in: Jpurnal of Financial Compliance, Vol. 8, No. 1, pp. 32–42.

Glaser, Christian (2022b): Digitale Transformation im Bankenumfeld—Zukunftsfähige Prozesse und Technologien erfolgreich implementieren, damit die Digitalisierung gelingt, Wiesbaden, pp. 299–317.

Glaser, Christian (2022a): Risikomanagement im Leasing—Grundlagen, rechtlicher Rahmen und praktische Umsetzung, Wiesbaden, pp. 1–14.

Gorobet, Ilinca (2023): Convergence of banking cybersecurity strategies to the new rules on digital operational resilience, in: Academy of Economic Studies of Moldova—Proceedings of International Conference, pp. 54–63.

Grima, Simon/Marano, Pierpaolo (2021): Designing a Model for Testing the Effectiveness of a Regulation: The Case of DORA for Insurance Undertakings, in: Risks, Vol. 9, No. 206.

Hackethal, Andreas/Inderst, Roman (2015): Auswirkungen der Regulatorik auf kleinere und mittlere Banken am Beispiel der deutschen Genossenschaftsbanken, Frankfurt.

Hellenkamp, Detlef (2025): Institutionelle Transformation im Bankensektor: Multidimensionale Analyse der Auswirkungen von Digitalisierung, ESG, Demografie und Regulierung auf deutsche und europäische Kreditinstitute, in: Diskussionspapier Duale Hochschule Baden-Württemberg, Stuttgart.

Hille, Lars (2018): Banken zwischen Regulierung und Digitalisierung—Geschäftsmodell unter Stress, in: Böhnke, Werner/Rolfes, Bernd (Eds.), Neue Erlösquellen oder Konsolidierung?—Geschäftsmodelle der Banken und Sparkassen auf dem Prüfstand—Beiträge des Duisburger Banken-Symposiums, Wiesbaden, pp. 62–83.

Igl, Andreas (2024): IKT-Risikomanagement unter DORA—Einbindung in ICAAP und ILAAP, in: FIRM—Frankfurter Institut für Risikomanagement und Regulierung.

Janciute, Laima (2025): Cybersecurity in the financial sector and the quantum-safe cryptography transition: in search of a precautionary approach in the EU Digital Operational Resilience Act framework, in: International Cybersecurity Law Review, Vol. 6, pp. 145–154.

Janssen, Marus/Schreier, Margit/Stamann, Christoph (2016): Qualitative Inhaltsanalyse—Versuch einer Begriffsbestimmung und Systematisierung, in: Forum: Qualitative Sozialforschung, Vol. 17, No.3, Art. 16.

Joosen, Bart/Lehmann, Matthias (2019): Proportionality in the Single Rule Book, in: Chiti, Mario/Santro, Vittorio (Eds.), The Palgrave Handbook of European Banking Union Law, Cham, pp. 65–90.

Kourmpetis, Stavros (2022): Management of ICT Third Party Risk Under the Digital Operational Resilience Act, in: Böffel, Lukas/Schürger, Jonas (Eds.), Digitalisation, Sustainability, and the Banking and Capital Markets Union—Thoughts on Current Issues of EU Financial Regulation, Cham, pp. 211–226.

Kudinova, Alina/Maslii, Oleksandra/Smokvina, Valerii/Tsyhanenko, Kyryl (2025): The Impact of digitalization on the Financial Institutions' Economic Security in the Face of Growing Cyber Threats, in: Financial & Credit Activity: Problems of Theory & Practice, Vol. 4, No. 63, pp. 466–483.

Kun, Eyup (2024): Challenges in regulating cloud service providers in EU financial regulation: From operational to systemic risks, and examining challenges of the new oversight regime for critical cloud service providers under the Digital Operational Resilience Act, in: Coomputer Law & Cybersecurity Review: The International Joural of Technology Law and Practice, Vol.52, pp. 1–15.

Leusmann, Klaus (2023): Nachhaltig erfolgreiches Bankmanagement—Ein Paradigmenwechsel für Banksteuerung und Bankenregulierung, Wiesbaden, pp. 73–88.

Milkau, Udo (2021): Operational resilience as a new concept and extension of operational risk management, in: Journal of Risk Management in Financial Institutions, Vol.14, No. 4, pp. 408–425.

Mulligan, James/Pierides, Mike (2024): Key themes of resiliency, outsourcing and third-party risk management regimes, in: Journal of Securities Operations & Custody, Vol 17, No. 2, pp. 102–118.

Mwai, Rose/ Ogada, Ken/Wabala, Samuel (2023): Role of ICT Risk Management on Insider Fraud Prevention in Commercial Banks in Nairobi County, in: International Journal of Technology and Systems, Vol. 8, No.3, pp. 36–64.

Ositashvili, Magda (2024): The key role of the most recent EU regulation—the "Digital Operational Resilence Act" in the legal system, contemporary challenges, and Georgian perspectives, in: European Scientific Journal, Vol. 20, No. 26, pp. 1–20.

Osman, Yasmin (2024): Basiswissen Bankenaufsicht: Von Abwicklung bis Zinsrisiko—so werden Banken überwacht, Stuttgart, 2. Auflage.

Perera, Patricia (2018): Operational risk management: the basel II, in: Instituto Superior de Contabilidade e Administração do Instituto Politécnico, Porto.

Petersen, Christoph (2012): Laterale Technologietransferprojekte in multinationalen Unternehmen—Methodik der empirischen Untersuchung, Wiesbaden, pp. 137–174.

Pier-Giorgio, Chiara (2024): Towards a right to cybersecurity in EU law? The challenges ahead, in: Computer Law & Security Review, Vol. 53.

Priller, Markus (2025): DORA in Versicherungsunternehmen—Regulatorik, Vorgehensmodell, praktische Aspekte, Erfolgsfaktoren, Karlsruhe, pp. 163–218.

Rani, Nanda/Saha, Bikash/Shukla, Kumar (2025): Generative AI in Financial Institution: A Global Survey of Opportunities, Threats, and Regulation, o.O.

Reinert, Nicolas (2018): Die Europäische Bankenaufsicht—Auswirkungen auf regional ausgerichtete Institute, in: Böhnke, Werner/Rolfes, Bernd (Eds.), Neue Erlösquellen oder Konsolidierung?—Geschäftsmodelle der Banken und Sparkassen auf dem Prüfstand—Beiträge des Duisburger Banken-Symposiums, Wiesbaden, pp. 62–83.

Resano, Jose Ramon (2022): Digital resilience and financial stability. The quest for policy tools in the financial sector, in: Financal Stability Review, Vol.43, pp. 57–82

Riaz, Bilal/Younas, Zeeshan (2024): Investigating the impact of DORA Regulations on Third Party Risk Management in the Swedish Financial Sector, Stockholm.

Rocholl, Jörg et al. (2017): Bankenmarkt: Droht ein neuer Deregulierungswettbewerb mit Risiken für die europäischen Banken?, in: ifo Schnelldienst, Vol. 70, No. 1, pp. 3–18.

Scheidl, Marcus (2023): Neue Anforderungen an IKT-Infrastrukturen im Finanzsektor, in: FIRM News, No. 1, pp. 1–4.

Schlenker, Ben/Waschbusch, Gerd (2024): Geteiltes Wissen, gestärkte Resilienz: Informationsaustausch über Cyberbedrohungen gemäß Art. 45 DORA, in: International Cybersecurity Law Review, Vol. 5, pp. 213–236.

Scott, Hal (2021): The E.U.'s Digital Operational Resilience Act: Cloud Services & Financial Companies, in: Program on International Financial Systems—Havard Law School.

Siems, Thomas (2025): Do Banking Regulations Disproportionately Impact Smaller Community Banks?, in: Conference of State Bank Supervisors (CSBS).

Socrates, Majune (2017): A concise Review of classical linear Regression Model Assumptions with Practice using Stata, o.O.

Sowa, Aleksandra (2025): Meldepflichten für Sicherheitsvorfälle, Vorfälle und IKT-bezogene Vorfälle—Getrennt oder Zusammen?, in: Datenschutz und Datensicherheit, Vol. 1, pp. 48–54.

Teichmann, Fabian (2025): Ransomware extortion in Europe: legal responses and mitigation strategies, in: International Cybersecurity Law Review, Vol. 6, pp. 253–285.

Wendt, Stefan (2024): Informationsregister: Die unterschätzte DORA-Hürde, in: FIRM—Frankfurter Institut für Risikomanagement und Regulierung.

Wolberg, Hans-Bernd (2020): SREP—Neues Prüfungskonzept der Bankenaufsicht, in: Rolfes, Bernd/Wessling, Holger (Eds.), Complexity Kills—Banken im Dickicht von Regulierung und verkrusteten Strukturen—Beiträge des Duisburger Banken-Symposiums, Wiesbaden, pp. 54–67.